S0-BIG-689

A Millstone Round My Neck

Also by Norman Thelwell

Angels on Horseback
Thelwell Country
Thelwell in Orbit
A Place of Your Own
A Leg at Each Corner
Thelwell's Riding Academy
Top Dog
Up the Garden Path
The Compleat Tangler
Thelwell's Book of Leisure
This Desirable Plot
The Effluent Society
Penelope
Three Sheets in the Wind
Belt Up
Thelwell Goes West
Thelwell's Brat Race
Thelwell's Gymkhana
A Plank Bridge by a Pool

NORMAN THELWELL

A Millstone Round My Neck

EYRE METHUEN · LONDON

First published in 1981
by Eyre Methuen Ltd
11 New Fetter Lane, London EC4P 4EE
Copyright © Norman Thelwell 1981
ISBN 0 413 48300 2
Printed in Hampshire, England
by BAS Printers Ltd, Over Wallop, Stockbridge
and bound in Cornwall, England
by Robert Hartnoll Ltd, Bodmin

Contents

The Mill at Penruin

The old blue Rover nosed its way between the high Cornish banks draped with pennywort and trembling primroses. We could not see the surrounding countryside except for occasional glimpses of sunlit fields as we passed by gateways recessed deeply into the overgrown walls. It was unnerving to drive along these slotted lanes where two cars could not pass and endless convolutions hid the road ahead. A stoat ran across, a small dark snake-like creature against the sunlit surface, and was gone. A buzzard rose suddenly from the hedge-topped wall on the left. They were the only signs of life. The drone of low gears was monotonous.

There was an air of unreality about the situation. There we were, driving through remote country, looking for a water-mill. Twenty-four hours before we had not known of its existence. My wife, Rhona, had been reading the Sunday papers when she said suddenly, 'Would you like a picturesque water-mill in Cornwall with a three bedroomed cottage attached and all ripe for modernization? It's in a delightful wooded valley,' she added, reading on, 'with its own stretch of salmon and trout river, mill leat, cider-press and range of outbuildings. Needs some attention.'

I read the item over myself several times. 'How long would it take to pack for a few days holiday?' I asked.

'About an hour,' said my wife, dashing upstairs. 'We could start early in the morning before the traffic gets heavy.' And we did.

A dark tyre mark ahead turned abruptly to the left and disappeared into the bank. 'There's another gate coming up,' I said. 'I'll pull in.'

'You might as well,' said my wife. 'I think we're lost.' She was sitting beside me fumbling with the folds of an Ordnance map. I slowed to a crawl and edged the car into the gap. It was shallow and one side of the car was still on the road surface when I switched off the engine.

'I'll nip out and try to find out where we are,' I said. The field beyond the twisted metal gate was a dazzling carpet of lush green grass occupied by a herd of black-faced sheep. They were all standing, heads erect, and staring at me transfixed as if a moonship had just landed amongst them. A moth-eaten animal near the gate with bulging eyes and legs atremble emitted a tremulous bleat and the whole herd thundered away in panic up the slope and over the hill. There was nothing to see but the spring grass and pale blue sky.

'Can't see a thing,' I said, getting back into the car and starting the engine.

'Look out,' screamed my wife. A scarlet blur came round the corner only yards ahead, going like a red hot bolt. We gripped the dashboard with white knuckles and ducked our heads. There was a loud swishing noise and a metallic click. The car rocked gently in a funnel of rushing air. Through the rear window we glimpsed the back of a small GPO van as it disappeared round a corner. I emerged shakily to assess the damage. Clumps of coarse grass, moss and pale primrose stars were scattered along the road as if fired from a cannon. Several feet of the opposite bank were scoured clean of vegetation and the bare stones exposed to the light like bones in a fearful wound. The car was undamaged save for a blood-like clot of paint on the corner of the rear bumper. I pulled out of the gateway as quickly as possible and we ground slowly on up the hill with knitted brows and knotted stomach muscles, sounding the horn every few yards like a demented bull. Five minutes later we emerged into a wider lane.

'That's better,' I said. 'It's wide enough for a bus here.'

'Don't *say* things like that,' whimpered my wife, straining backwards in her seat. 'Let's find a decent road before we meet another kamikaze driver.'

We did at last find a wider road and dropped down suddenly into a pretty village of white cottages clinging to the steep sides of a wooded valley. Through the valley a river rippled over boulders beneath the arches of a stone bridge and a pub nestled beside it with tables scattered on a small lawn near the water's edge. We crossed the bridge and came to a cottage on the corner of a side turning. There were postcards and other items displayed in its tiny windows and a postbox set in the white-washed wall flashed scarlet as if the building had been struck a glancing blow by the GPO van as it rocketed away into the surrounding lanes. The words 'Tregallion Post Office' were painted above the door. 'I'll call in and tell them what I think of their postman,' I said, bringing the car to a halt.

'You'll do no such thing,' said my wife. 'They're touchy in Cornwall about foreigners from across the Tamar River. Do you want to start a feud before we find the mill? Calm down,' she added, glancing at her reflection in the mirror on the sun visor. She patted her hair and smoothed her rumpled coat. 'If anyone knows the way to this mill it should be the local postmistress,' she said, with maddening logic. We pushed open the cottage door and a bell on a coiled spring jangled loudly overhead, reminding me vividly of the corner sweetshop I knew as a child. A little old lady with hair as silver as the rims of her spectacles emerged from behind a red velvet curtain in the corner. She hovered attentively as we turned the squeaking display stand round and round, admiring the local views. We selected a card.

'Could you possibly direct us to Penruin Mill?' asked my wife, hugging the card and waiting for me to fumble for three pennies.

'You interested in old Garvey's place, my dear?' the old lady squeaked with obvious interest. 'Hubby a miller?' she added, with a grin that brought her chin dangerously near to her nose.

'No,' I said, trying to look amused. 'We hear it's for sale and thought we'd take a look.'

'It's just up the lane, midears,' she said, indicating the side turning. 'Can't miss it.'

We thanked her and the bell jangled again as we went out. 'Watch out for the surgeon,' she called as we closed the door.

'Who the hell's the surgeon?' I said as I started the engine and turned into the narrow lane.

'Whoever he is, I hope we don't meet him coming the other way in a car,' said Rhona, adjusting her safety belt. It was white-knuckle-time again. There was about one foot of space on each side of the car and the road appeared to rise at about forty-five degrees. The lane turned gently to the right so that we could see only a few yards ahead as we inched upwards. To the right was the familiar high bank and the land to the left, edged with coarse grass and scattered trees, fell sharply away to the river below. We passed the roof and chimneys of a cottage but hardly dared to glance at them. Gradually the road moved away from the river and the valley side became less steep. At the top it flattened out into a slightly wider surface and swung left, parallel to the river which was now hidden from view by trees. I eased the car into third gear and we came suddenly upon a long barn and, beyond it, a rather elaborate white gate which hinted at more prosperous days now gone. It lay open against the wall and gave access to a picturesque farmyard surrounded by stone buildings. A black and white sheepdog lay in the centre of the yard, dozing in the sunshine. He raised his head and watched us suspiciously, then laid his head along his paws again, leaving his ears still pricked. A few yards further along the

lane a narrow track dropped away down the slope towards the river. There was another wooden gate here, emerald with mosses and lying back in the tangled vegetation. It was as colourful as an ancient peeling fresco but, like so many treasures textured by time, one felt it would crumble to dust if disturbed. On an old piece of board at its foot, half overgrown with grass, the words 'Penruin Mill' were faintly discernible. We had found the mill at last.

We turned down the slope between walls of random granite which sprouted dark, tangled hedges at the tops. The tyres rumbled over big stones worn smooth by generations of iron-shod wagons and horses' hooves. The hedges ceased abruptly about halfway down the slope and we saw the mill.

It lay before us in the wooded valley like a long-awaited toy at the foot of the bed on Christmas morning. It was small and compact and had that perfection of shape and proportion so often seen in buildings which architects refer to as 'functional': buildings erected in a certain place for a certain reason. It was built of granite under a roof of greenish slate. A patina of mosses and ferns softened the grey stone and gemmed the wooden arms of the great wheel which curved against the wall and dipped into a trough, where its lower edge was tightly held by silt and loose boulders. Saplings grew there, their roots in the streamy water and their branches tangled in the rotting arms of the wheel. The paddles too were fretted to abstract shapes by dripping water and each held a little garden of grass, moss and ferns, like a display of window boxes. In the water below, a shoal of small brown trout held uncertain station, flicking forwards and dropping back endlessly against the narrow current, only inches from the mill walls. With its cluster of outbuildings the mill seemed to have grown there by the river, sprung up naturally from the rocky ground like the trees and flower-speckled grass around it, becoming part of the landscape and enriching it with its presence.

The mill was surrounded by three small paddocks and an orchard full of hoary lichen-hung apple trees. The mill-stream bubbled and gurgled its urgent way across the fields through

clumps of waving weed and water-cress and shattered into a foam of dancing white beads on the lip of the millrace. It fell through the wheel in a glittering cascade, raced through the tangled trough and disappeared below the yard to reappear again in the orchard beyond, where it was joined by two more little springs before turning at the further boundary and emptying once more into the river.

On the right-hand side of the yard a cider-press stood in an open-fronted building and fat barrels lay along the walls. Millstones and staddle stones were strewn about like confetti at a village wedding. Monolithic slabs of stone were everywhere, holding up a roof, supporting a gate or bridging the streams at crossing points. The orchard and paddocks were surrounded by Cornish banks, busy with nesting birds and studded with the bright stars of thousands of primroses. Wild daffodils danced and trembled among the apple trees and the air was alive with the music of running water. Across the little field beyond the mill a dipper bobbed and curtsied on the mossy boulders in the roaring, tumbling river. The wide-eyed enchantment of childhood was everywhere about us as if we had pushed open a little door into a magic garden.

The mill itself seemed packed with machinery. The deep shade of the interior, made darker by the instant change from clean spring sunshine, dissolved slowly in the light from the open doorway. As our eyes became adjusted to the gloom we saw the dust-caked floor and walls and the massive wooden beams. Standing there among the great gears and levers was like a childhood dream of strange exploration in the interior of some giant pocket-watch. On the far wall an open wooden staircase led to the second storey where the millstones still lay in their wooden casings beneath chutes and hoppers and a welter of mysterious paraphernalia of the milling trade. Another stairway led to the top room which was roofed with massive beams and random slabs of heavy slate. More wheels and levers were here and a morass of cogs and pulleys draped with sagging belts and ropes. It was all rich and beautiful and tinged with an aura of mediaeval menace.

Some of the small windows were broken and the half door swung loosely on its hinges. A variety of smaller cobwebbed implements of metal and wood stood about the floors, and the walls were draped with metal rims and heavy chains. Here and there small hand tools and a glove were placed as if laid down for a moment and never taken up again. There was an air about the whole building of sudden abandonment in the moment of some nameless catastrophy. Outside the sun beat down in the warm angle of the yard and the birds were noisy. Sparrows twittered on the gutters and a wren flew in at the open door and was lost in the dark recesses above the gears.

Attached to the mill and under the same greenish slate roof was the cottage with a cow byre beyond. This section of the edifice was more derelict than the mill itself but, although small, was equally massive in construction. The walls were two feet thick and up to three feet thick in places. The front door, flimsy by comparison, creaked open to our push. Inside was a tiny hallway which led on the left to a small sittingroom with a shuttered window and tiny glass-fronted cupboards on either side of the fireplace. The stone surround had been painted and a small Victorian grate built in. Pieces of worn lino lay about the floor and an old newspaper with twigs upon it filled the grate. In the midst of the neglect there remained a touch of faded elegance, for the window seat and glass-fronted cupboards, the panelled shutters and the sunlit prospect of the valley, hinted at tea in the parlour on Sunday afternoons when the wheel had stopped its rumbling.

Across the hallway was a big, square livingroom like a farm kitchen, covered on walls and ceiling with peeling flowered wallpaper. As in the small parlour, a big open fireplace with granite surrounds had been filled in with an iron range. It was red with rust and littered with bird droppings and the debris of neglected years. We had just such an iron range in the terraced house where I was born but it had been jet black with Zebo polish and my mother's elbow-grease. Each moulded edge had been buffed with emery cloth, producing lines of bright silver which glittered in the firelight as the kettle hissed on the coals behind the fireguard. I wondered whether the miller's wife had removed the iron oven shelves and wrapped them in paper to warm the beds on cold winter nights as my mother did. And did his children stub their toes also as they turned in warm sleep?

The ceiling, supported by a few widely-spaced beams, sagged ominously. A square hole had been sawn in the centre, revealing a dim bedroom above. We wondered often about that hole, for it had clearly been made for a purpose. Was it to bypass the narrow staircase in the restricted hall, so that furniture could be hauled up or down from the room above? It seemed too small for that. What then? Perhaps the miller himself was pulled up to bed through it when the local cider had made the stairs too hazardous. But what, we thought, if he staggered out of bed in the night with a hole like that in the floor? We never did solve the mystery of that yawning gap although it intrigues us still.

On the far side of the room a low doorway led on into a lean-to scullery through a wall almost three feet thick. There was a small window there which looked across the field towards the river and beneath it a deep, white ceramic sink with a tap stood on brick supports. The outer door of random-width planks opened directly into the field, for there was no garden and the woody stems of last summer's nettles bunched against the granite walls. Between these two main rooms and below the staircase in the hallway was another door to an old pantry. Heavy slate slabs formed shelving along one wall and iron hooks were fixed into the ceiling. A great bath, hewn from a single block of granite, stood in the corner. The place had a distinctly sinister air. We stood in the doorway, peering.

'It's the old pig room,' I said brightly, 'where they used to scald the hide off the carcase when preparing the bacon and hams before they could get packets of frozen rubbish from the village store. You see those hooks?' But my wife had gone. I found her in the big livingroom staring up at the hole in the ceiling. 'We could soon get those hooks out of there,' I said, 'and the stone bath would be lovely outside the front door, full of rock plants. When it was cleared it would make a lovely spare bedroom.' I was about to ask, 'What do you think?' but decided not to.

She was still staring up at the hole in the ceiling when I suggested that we should explore upstairs. I took her hand and we mounted the creaking boards gingerly. The bones of my fingers were almost crushed by the time we reached the little landing. There was a small bedroom to the left with a window which looked out along the wall of the mill. 'Make a perfect bathroom,' I muttered as we shuffled out. I hoped she hadn't seen the black stain on the ceiling. There was a larger bedroom beyond, attractively irregular in shape. A little window by the chimney breast looked out along the mill-stream and another, with its own window-seat, overlooked the river field. I was relieved to see how normal it looked – even charming.

On the other side of the landing was the room above the hole. The door was slightly ajar and I stepped inside. Rhona grabbed at my jacket. 'Don't go in there,' she pleaded. 'The floor might give way.' I took another step to show how little I cared for such fancies. The room was square and featureless except for a window with a seat below, recessed into the thick wall. I could see the steep path climbing back to the road above and the russet swell of the moors beyond. It was a picture of sunlit rural richness distorted here and there by the undulating glass. There was no doubt that the hole did look unnerving and I turned back to the door. Bird droppings and a profusion of owl pellets – regurgitated by some soft-feathered hunter of the lonely hours, who used it as a vantage point from which to watch and listen for unwary mice – were scattered below its outer edge. I was glad that my wife asked no questions as we went downstairs.

In several places in the lower rooms the rain had found its way inside the walls and fed large mounds of moss like cushions of bottle-green velvet on the damp plaster. The floors were paved with large slabs of Delabole slate, and all were cracked, broken and ingrained with dirt. We had not expected to find the place in good order, but there was an air of desolation within which was depressing. We returned to the scullery where the sun slanted through the window and patterned the old sink.

I opened the door again and the warm sunshine flooded in, glowing on the dusty red tiles and reflecting a warm orange light about us. We leaned against the door jamb and looked at the view. The green hillsides glittered and the smell of clean growing countryside revived our spirits. The valley stretched away before us. A pair of bullfinches were busy in a clump of willows by the little gate which led to the kitchen garden beyond the cow byre. Across the river the green hillsides were patterned with grazing cattle and sheep and a buzzard circled lazily in the high, powder-blue dome of the sky. My wife looked across at me with the faint smile of one who accepts the inevitable but does not really mind.

We collected our lunch from the car, found some old boxes in the cowshed and picnicked by the river. We disturbed a heron that rose from the water's edge and beat slowly away downstream, but he served only to emphasize the drowsy solitude. By the time we had eaten and repacked the car we had decided to have a talk with the owner who lived in the farm at the top of the hill. We drove back up the steep track from the mill yard to the road above and were soon turning into the farmyard where we had seen the dog earlier

that day. He was nowhere to be seen but I am not easily fooled by farm dogs, having had some experience of them in the past. I peered into all the recesses of the yard, therefore, before opening the car door. It was open only an inch or two when he streaked from the farmhouse door and leaped at the car with such velocity that the door slammed shut again, almost trapping my fingers. Barking madly, he pawed at the window and scraped the paintwork with harsh claws. Many animal lovers, I am sure, would have wound down the window cooing, 'Who's a lovely dog then?' and invited him to rasp the skin of their faces with his tongue, but not me. I revved the engine violently in a mechanical cry for help.

A tall, thin woman in a dark dress and loose woollen cardigan appeared at the door. She strode across and hauled the animal off by the scruff of his neck, fetching him a sharp crack across his head. He slunk away with a sidelong glance from his wall-eye as we emerged from the car.

'He wouldn't hurt you really,' she said, ignoring the deep tracks down the paintwork. 'He's just a bit boisterous.'

After we had explained our reason for calling she introduced herself as Mrs Garvey and led us into the farmhouse. We entered a shadowy hall with a big oak dresser full of pewter and brass ornaments against the wall and two quaint red and white pottery lions beneath it on the slate floor. A black grandfather clock, heavily carved and with the sun and moon painted on its face and a slowly swinging pendulum behind a glass panel, ticked timelessly by the staircase. She showed us into a big square room and asked us if we would like some tea. We said we would like some very much and she went away to make it, her footsteps disappearing into the stillness of the house. We stared about us in silence.

The room was only slightly lighter than the hall we first entered. It had a high moulded ceiling and wooden panelling halfway up the walls. There were some pieces of dark, heavy furniture. A profusion of stuffed birds and animals stood about on side tables or were fixed to the faded wallpaper above the panels. Over the fireplace a fox, with one paw stiffly raised, held a long-dead partridge in its mouth – a rigormortis tableau in a glass-fronted coffin. There was a faint air of faded prosperity in the room which echoed the message of the sagging but ornate front gate to the farmyard. Its story of steady dissolution was reinforced by the rumpled carpet and shabby armchairs in which we sat.

There seemed little we could say to each other. A whispered word seemed like an offence in the silence. There was a sudden scrabble and scratching on the hall floor and the dog burst in. Pausing only to send Rhona's handbag flying in the air, he leapt upon me like a bear, panting and ramming his wet muzzle into my face. He had skinned my nose and scraped two buttons off my jacket when Mrs Garvey entered with the teatray. She placed it carefully upon the table before swiping the dog's head with a napkin. He flew out of the door and thudded heavily into the dresser, setting the brass and pewter rattling. Some nameless metal disc crashed to the floor and spun round and round on the ringing stone until it settled into silence.

Mrs Garvey smiled. 'He's taken to you, Mr T.,' she said, 'and he doesn't take to everyone. But he's a bit boisterous. You need a dog that's a bit boisterous when you live out here.' We sipped our tea while Mrs Garvey explained that she did not deal with business matters herself any more but that all her affairs were now dealt with by 'Surgey' (that enigmatic name again). He was, she said, a great man, an eminent surgeon and a war hero who had fought with the resistance forces in Yugoslavia. She hinted at great figures of the war years and key events in which he had been concerned. Surgey was in bed at that moment, she explained. 'He has a lot of trouble with shrapnel, you know. It keeps moving about,' but he would be up in about half an hour and if we cared to return to the mill he would meet us there shortly. We thanked her for her hospitality and made haste to the car before the dog could intercept us.

We explored the cider-press and the cluster of outhouses on the other side of the mill yard while we waited, but our minds were not really on them. Who was he, this distinguished surgeon, this great soldier of noble bearing, we wondered, and would we hear him coming as the shrapnel moved about? It was little wonder that the postmistress had warned us to watch out for him. I had spent some years in the infantry myself and had met a fair number of high-ranking officers it had been advisable to watch out for.

We were looking at a tiny spring which bubbled up among the wild daffodils in the orchard when a small figure appeared beside us. He was obviously a farm worker of the old school – shabbily dressed and his face deeply lined by years of harsh work and worse weather. His hands were rough with labour and his battered hat looked as if it had been used for a variety of purposes, including cleaning out the stables.

'Mr T?' he asked, proffering a gnarled hand. 'You vish to talk about zer mill, yes? I am Surgey.' I had once met a big, red-faced bearded man in a peaked cap and fisherman's jersey, sitting on an upturned boat at Looe. He was selling sharks' teeth and coral. 'Ow goes it, Whack?' he had said to me in a broad Liverpool accent, and I have been sceptical of local characters ever since. But Surgey was a class above the Scotland Road skipper. Some minutes later we stood in the mill once more among the welter of machinery, with the sun slanting through a tiny window like a spotlight in the motey air. Surgey was lit up like a puppet on a ramshackle stage. He had extracted a rusty penknife from his pocket and was stabbing the huge timbers as if to demonstrate their solid strength.

The mill had not been mentioned since he introduced himself in the orchard. He had walked a little ahead of us with his head down like an usher and talked continuously in his thick mid-European accent. As far as we could tell it had all been information about himself – about the past – about the war – but all in vague, incomplete statements which left us floundering. He shifted his stabbing action to short overarm jabs. 'I vos zer greatest surgeon in my country – Tito is my friend – zer Germans, it vos terrible – your Mr Churchill vos my friend – he keep ze Spitfire engine running all zer time if I should need it. Ah! zose days ve do not talk about.'

'Have you been in England long?' I ventured. He left the penknife trembling in the woodwork.

'But of course zis iss my country now – Mrs Garvey is so kind I manage all her business but zer shrapnel still comes out.' We glanced apprehensively at the floor but there was nothing near his wellingtons.

'How much are you asking for the mill?' I asked.

'Eet is beautiful. Yes?' he said, trying to extract his penknife without success. He struggled for a moment or two then placed his boot against the beam and tugged with both hands. It shot out and he staggered back a few paces. 'Zey don't build zem like zis any more,' he said, looking directly at us. 'Five sousand pounts.'

I knew at that moment that whatever else he might be, he was certainly no fool. I had an uneasy feeling that he might recount the whole episode later in a perfect Cornish cream accent to Mrs Garvey, as she dabbed tears of laughter from her eyes or, even worse, retail it in the pub for years to come whilst the locals cried into their beer. I offered four thousand. He didn't haggle, simply slipped back into the past. 'Ze conditions in vich I haf operated ver terrible,' he muttered, scoring long lines down the oak with his rusty blade. Whether the operations were military or surgical, or both, he did not explain. 'I vil talk with Mrs Garvey, poor lady,' he said. 'I do not sink four and a half sousand but I vil talk viz 'er.'

We left shortly after that, having agreed to meet again next morning and with the vague idea that he 'vud talk viz Mrs Garvey, poor lady'. We said that we would also talk about it together, but that four thousand pounds was more than we had planned to spend.

He was still operating on the oak beams when we left the mill and drove away to find a hotel for the night.

The next morning we returned to the farmhouse and, after an hour or so of wartime reminiscences interspersed with occasional references to the mill, Surgey suddenly agreed that our third final offer of £4,250 was a fair price. He sprang to his feet. 'In Cornval ve haf ze tradition,' he said. 'Ve slap ze hants.' I held up my hand and he gave it a lusty blow. 'Now you gif me ze shillink,' he said. I gave him a shilling. 'Zer is only now ze fifty pounts for Mrs Garvey, poor lady, and ve haf sealed ze bargain.' I had no idea what he was talking about, but the sudden end to our strange negotiations had rather thrown me. No doubt Old Cornish Traditions interpreted by an ex-Balkan freedom fighter were bound to be a bit obscure. So I said nothing.

The next day I parted with a cheque for £50 extra for Mrs

Garvey, poor lady, which was wheedled out of me by some devious argument which I have never been able to follow to this day. As I was a little alarmed at Surgey's colourful description of what my newly-acquired acres would look like if they were not immediately grazed, I had assured him that I would be grateful if he would put his sheep and bullocks upon them forthwith.

He did not mention any rent for the grazing rights. I was nervous of doing so because I felt sure that if rent were decided upon, it would be me who would be called upon to pay it. It was naive of me, however, to think that I was going to get away with things as easily as that. Hardly had I returned my cheque book to the safety of my pocket and agreed that he should treat the property more or less as his own, when he said, 'Zere is zer matter of zer fertilizer of course.' I suppose that I must have betrayed my lack of agricultural know-how because Mrs G., who had been sitting silently in the background throughout our discussion, leapt in to explain this new item.

'He thinks,' she said, 'that the land needs a dressing of fertilizer before he puts the beasts upon it. It is in poor heart, you see, and the bullocks will poach it.' If these technical terms were designed to confuse me, they were well chosen. I had never heard of bullocks poaching things before.

'Zer bullocks poach it viz zer feet,' put in Surgey by way of clarification.

'They press the fertilizer into the ground with their feet,' added Mrs G. 'So it's important to spread it before the animals go on to it.' I was beginning to see the light. 'Surgey wants to know whether you have any objections to him going ahead straight away with the fertilizer,' she explained.

'Not at all,' I said. 'Please do if you think it is needed.'

'Sank you,' said Surgey. 'If you will let me have forty pounts I sink it vil be enough.' I was beginning to feel sorry for any Germans who had been foolish enough to tangle with him when he had been fighting on his own ground.

'I'll think about it,' I said, moving towards the door. 'Incidentally, does anyone poach the river?' It was a throwaway shaft of wit designed to throw him off the scent of my wallet.

'I'm afraid you vil have zis trouble,' he said, warming to the subject in a flash. 'But I vil valk zer river vis zer dog and ve vil see zem off. If you vil let me have. . .' But we were out of the room and hurrying through the hall as fast as the dog's low growls would permit.

We hurried away to admire our new property. It was a morning of sheer delight. The air was as clear and potent as cider, the sunshine as soft as cream. Twenty-four hours ago we had never set eyes on the place and now it was ours. We were in love with it all: the crusty stone walls, the warm green slate and the pennywort and tiny ferns which nestled in each crevice. The lichen on the green apple boughs was more luxuriant, more colourful than any we had seen before, the daffodils were brighter and the primroses more innocent than we had known. We walked beside the streams and shaded our eyes against the dazzle of their wavelets and sat beside the river listening to it roar. The birds sang counter-point to the water in a pastorale. We stood for a while beside the tiny spring which bubbled like soda water from beneath a rock in the orchard. It was mine now, that spring. The water and the bubbles were mine and, although they did not know it, the tiny brown trout flicking among the stones and the caddis fly there on the smooth white pebble, trundling his own property upon his back, were mine too. His house was like the mill, built of stones neatly cemented together, functional and beautiful. He had built it himself and not acquired it as I had done with a slap of the hand and a shilling.

There was no really reliable water supply to the cottage in spite of the tap at the scullery sink, but we need worry about that no longer for had we not a constant supply of clear water, unpolluted by injections of fluoride and other additives? We had only to arrange for this nectar to be piped beneath the daffodils and we could live as man was meant to live, drinking the pure water of the hills. A rustling noise from the tangled hedge above us on the slope broke through our thoughts. We looked up to see a black and white head regarding us with big patient eyes beneath long lashes. The cow's jaw stopped for a moment and then resumed its gentle, rhythmic chewing.

A brilliant blue point of light volplaned towards us from the field beyond the hedge and lit on a thin hawthorn wand not ten feet away from us. The kingfisher was clearly in focus for perhaps ten seconds as his claws grasped the swaying twig, then he was gone, a tracer bullet of colour whistling down the slope to the river. I felt quite guilty that I should ever have haggled over the monetary value of such an earthly paradise.

We returned to Hampshire in a state of euphoria. It was spring and I owned a watermill. There was work to do of course but what a pleasure it would be to organize such a worthwhile job. What a transformation there would be by the time the daffodils were blowing once more by the orchard spring.

The old blue Rover seemed to skim along like a bird as we drove back eastwards over the sunlit moors.

The Grand Design

A week or two later we returned to Tregallion to seek out a local builder who was willing to carry out the work I wanted done at the mill and I was introduced to a local artisan who claimed to have intimate knowledge of Penruin. He lived at Pollen, a tiny village about two miles away, and promptly called round to see me to talk things over. He was a remarkable character of about middle height, not fat but with enough paunch to overhang his trouser belt in a comfortable way. He wore a bowler hat which had once been black but had matured to a sludgy green colour. The brim had become detached from the crown round three-quarters of its circumference so that it trembled across his forehead as he spoke. The sun shone through the gap and cast a moving yellow line across his face. He wore an old waistcoat, innocent of buttons, and a working shirt with a frayed collar which was open at the neck. From the right-hand point of the collar a clip-on bow tie hung vertically downward as if deliberately placed there to complete his ensemble.

He had known the mill since he was a boy, he said, and had a man on his staff who had worked there when the wheel was turning and the stones were grinding out flour – or was it the man's father? He wasn't quite sure. However, it was a sin and a shame to see the old place falling apart and he would be proud to restore it to its former glory; we had only to give him our instructions. Things were a little slack at the moment, he explained, and he was in a position to put the work in hand without delay. He handed me his card or, rather, a much folded and rather grubby letterhead which he fished out of his waistcoat pocket.

It read: 'J. Pretty, "Carpenter and Decorator.
Funerals furnished. Cremations arranged."'

I was pleased to notice that he was experienced in undertaking work which required immediate attention. I promised to return at an early date with an architect who would make a complete survey

of the buildings and draw up a schedule of work, so that he could give us an estimate of the costs involved and a fairly accurate idea of how long the work was likely to take. I thought his eyes rolled a little towards heaven when I mentioned the word architect but he managed a reassuring smile. He promised to hold himself ready to meet us on site whenever it might be convenient to our good selves.

Don Chambers was an architect who had been employed most of his working life by a large brewery combine. His creative spirit had been frustrated by years of working on what he described as 'brewers' modern tat' and he was always glad to escape into work which gave him some freedom. With his help I had restored the Hampshire cottage which we lived in at that time and, when I told him about the watermill he offered to help me with that, too. Don wrote to Mr Pretty telling him that we would both be visiting Penruin on a certain date and asking him to meet us there for a general discussion about our plans. By making an early start on the appointed day we arrived on the site at about ten-thirty as arranged. The weather was good and Don was captivated by the mill from the moment he saw it. Before he started work with his measuring stick and notebook we wandered about the place waiting for the builder to join us. There was no sound but the bleating of distant sheep and the song of the birds. At half past eleven we gave up and started work in the cottage. Lunchtime came and went and we worked on without interruption. About three o'clock in the afternoon a sheep put its head in at the open door and bleated so loudly that I fell off the tea chest I was standing on. The crash obviously alarmed him for he disappeared as quickly as he came and we saw him no more. We saw no builder either, nor heard a bleat from him.

We had to start back by five o'clock if we are to get home that night but, as Mr Pretty lived only a mile or two away we made a slight detour and called on him at his cottage in Pollen. A big woman with red forearms and ample bosom answered the door and we explained our mission.

"'E don't work Saturdays,' she said.

'Do you know where he might be?' we enquired. She disappeared without a word and returned to the door a moment later.

'His golf bag's not in the cupboard,' she said. 'He'll be at the Green Dragon in Travellion, likely.' We thanked her and turned the car for home. . . .

About a week later I received a copy of a schedule of work which Don had dispatched by post to the builder, together with a letter couched in firm but professional jargon. He was 'disappointed', he said, that Mr Pretty had not met us on site as arranged and hoped that whatever emergency had prevented his appearance at the mill was now over. He trusted that such an unforeseen event would not happen again and asked that he give us an estimate of cost for the schedule of work enclosed with all speed. It was a neat and lengthy document and, in essence, covered the following points:

a. The testing by the local electricity board of all electric wiring and installations and the rectification of any faults therein. A list of new additional requirements was appended.
b. The public analyst was to take samples of the spring water with a view to pumping it to a new storage tank on the top floor of the mill.
c. A drainage system was to be installed to a septic tank not less than 50 yards from the northeast corner of the cowshed. All work was to be in accordance with local authority requirements and best local practice.
d. All necessary work to timbers and slates of the roof to be carried out with urgency to leave the roof watertight and weatherproof. All gutters and downspouts to be taken down, cleaned and replaced, using only first quality materials as specified for replacements where necessary.

There followed a precise and detailed specification of work to be carried out on each room of the cottage to restore it to a warm, dry habitation. The old plaster was to be hacked off and all piping and ducts necessary for a complete electricity and water system were to be installed before replastering commenced. The smallest bedroom was to be converted to a bathroom as detailed and the pig room cleared of all shelving, hooks and other appurtenances. The granite bath was to be removed and placed against the outside wall adjacent to the front door, and the floor relaid. All slate floors were to be removed and replaced with new blue stones of similar size. The fireplaces were to be cleared of all installations and obstructions, and the stonework and lintel beams cleaned and exposed as originally designed. A new front door was to be made and fitted. A neat, professional architect's drawing was included giving exact details of this item.

Ceilings and bedroom floors were to be inspected and all doubtful timber removed and replaced with new material. Beams were to be cleaned and any doubtful timber replaced with good quality oak; additional beams were to be added in the farm kitchen as specified to restore the bedroom floor to its original condition and the hole was to be filled in.

The final section of this schedule gave exact details of how the entire property was to be decorated when the preparatory work was approved by the architect and specified that all walls were to be lined with Kotina polystyrene thermal insulation sheet before final decoration commenced.

It was an admirable document, so detailed and exact that it was difficult to see how any snags could arise.

There now followed a maddening period when nothing happened. This was partly due, no doubt, to the fact that nothing ever seems to happen when the purchase of property reaches the stage where solicitors are involved. They can never find deeds and papers and things and then add insult to injury by charging search fees.

The builder must have taken up permanent residence at the Green Dragon. To be fair to the solicitors it seemed that they were up against it themselves. One letter contained the statement: 'It is difficult to persuade Cornish farm folk that there is any sense of urgency.'

It was high summer by the time purchase was completed and we had a reply from the builder. He was sorry, he wrote, that we had had a frustrating journey to meet him at the mill but he had not received any letter suggesting such a meeting. 'The post is a bit unreliable down here.' He trusted that we would find his enclosed estimate satisfactory and assured us that he had already committed his entire staff to the job in hand. 'You will be surprised,' he wrote, 'what a difference you will see in a few weeks time.' Don wrote back to him accepting his estimate and requesting that the work should now proceed with all possible speed. Two weeks later he made a surprise visit with his wife, Marion; apart from the fact that the front door was now off its hinges and there were some cow pats on the livingroom floor, nothing seemed to have changed. A careful search revealed no evidence that builders had passed that way. Surgey, however, was in the yard surveying a bunch of wild, unkempt bullocks, which were careering round the paddock. Don and Marion had not met him before but after introducing themselves to him, he had entertained them to a lengthy, if disjointed, account of his struggles against Hitler's hordes and run over his main achievements in the medical field.

He turned to Marion with a polite enquiry as to her own state of health. Unwisely, as it turned out, she replied that she was having trouble at the time with a suspected hiatus hernia. Surgey brightened visibly and before either of them knew what was happening he had undone two or three buttons on her blouse with his grubby fingers and was about to explore further when there was a cry of anguish from the lane above. It was Mrs Garvey. 'Surgey, come quickly!' she shouted. 'The sow's cut herself on some barbed wire.' He apologized to Marion for being called away before he had had time to make a full examination and disappeared up the hill.

Before they left to call upon the builder Surgey appeared in the yard again with an enamel jug and a length of plastic tubing. Marion jumped into the car, slammed the door and fastened her coat up to the neck. He asked Don if he would like to try the cider in the barrels by the press. A bit uncertain of how to proceed, Don said that he would. Surgey produced his rusty old pen knife, prised the bung out of a barrel and pushed the tube inside. He sucked on the other end until the colour started to drain from his face but without any other result. 'Zer tube is too bent,' he said. 'It vil not reach zer cider.' He rooted in the corner of the building and came up with a four-inch cut nail and a length of old binder string.

He tied the string to the nail and then to the plastic tubing and stuffed it all back into the bung hole. The weight of the nail must have straightened the tube a bit because when he resumed sucking, a stream of cider started to run. He directed the jet into a dusty old bottle from the motley collection along the top of the wall and handed it to Don before filling up his own jug. When he tried to extract the tube, the nail caught across the hole and all efforts to yank it out by force failed. He took out his penknife again and cut the string. The nail, with some of the string still tied to it, fell into the brew and Surgey hammered the wooden plug back into place.

Don explained that he could not risk drinking cider at that moment because he had yet to call upon the builder and then face a long drive home. Surgey quite understood. He produced a cork from his collection and the bottle was sealed and stowed safely away in the car boot before they set off to seek out Mr Pretty.

They met the builder in his yard, planing up a coffin lid. He was abject with apologies. He'd been waiting for the electricity board's report, he explained, and to hear from the public analyst about the spring water. 'You can't shift some of they, midear,' he said. 'I've been feeling a bit dickey myself, to tell the truth.' But he'd have his full team down at the mill the very next day, he assured Don, and *then* he'd see a difference.

'How did you get rid of the bottle of cider?' I asked. 'Did you pour it down the sink when you got home?'

'Well, not exactly,' said Don, 'I was just about to tip it away when curiosity got the better of me. I had a sip and then another . . . and another . . . It was soft as moss with a kick like a mule. After twenty years of working for a brewery I've never tasted anything so good.'

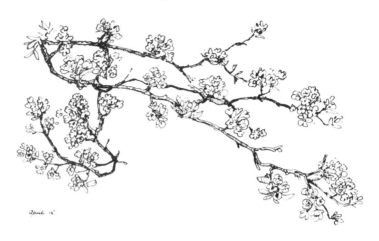

April 16.

Five weeks had passed since Don's visit to the mill and my work had kept me confined to my desk at home. It was now more than halfway through August and I could hardly wait to see what the mill looked like now that work had been under way for more than a month. But my brother Alan and his wife Kathleen were due to visit us for a couple of weeks with their two boys and there seemed little prospect of a trip to Cornwall for some time. When they arrived they brought Kath's mother and my father with them so we had a very full house.

I must admit that I made the most of my captive audience. I told them all about the place and explained in detail how we were making the cottage into a warm, comfortable home without sacrificing one jot of its character – how I intended to preserve the mill itself with all its machinery and restore the great water-wheel so that it would turn once more when the sluice gate was opened.

My own two children and their young cousins showed most interest in my descriptions of the pig room and were visibly excited by the details of the stone bath and iron hooks in the ceiling. I was forced to give them repeat descriptions behind the garden shed, however, because any mention of the subject in Rhona's presence seemed to disturb her. Her whole frame would stiffen instantly at the words 'pig room' and the accompanying pallor and tight closing of her eyes was reminiscent of the condition in which I sometimes found her in the bathroom at home; on these occasions I had learned to lead her gently but firmly out of the door and return with a rolled-up newspaper to deal with the spider in the bath. I would thump the side of the bath several times, bang on the walls and knock the soap rack on to the floor, then open and close the window noisily with a cheerful 'All clear, love.' When her head finally appeared round the door she would always express the hope that I had not hurt it. She wasn't keen on pursuing the mystery of the hole in the bedroom floor, either, since someone had suggested that it was probably for lowering a coffin to the pall-bearers below.

On the whole, however, my enthusiasm seemed to be infectious, particularly when I informed everyone that the cottage should now be well on the way to being weather-proof and if not exactly comfortable, then nearly so. I drew word pictures, too, of the cider-press and the barrels of potent scrumpy which lay beside it waiting for us to consume it at our leisure. I would be making my own, of course, from now on from my own apple orchard. It would be the real stuff. 'Soft as moss,' I said. 'And with a kick like a mule.'

'Why don't we go and see it while we're here?' asked Kath's mother. Everyone looked at me, waiting for an answer.

'There's no furniture in the place. No beds or chairs or tables, nothing,' I said.

'We don't mind,' said the children in unison. 'They won't have spoiled the pig room, will they?'

Mrs Woodier herself was no longer young – she was not in the best of health. 'We could rustle up enough camp beds for one night,' she said. 'It all sounds so lovely I can't wait to see it.'

'But it will take us six hours to get there,' I protested. 'Even if there are no traffic jams – which are quite likely in the middle of the holiday season. We would have to leave here by about five o'clock in the morning if we wanted to have a reasonable time there and avoid heavy traffic.'

'Lovely,' they all chorused. 'Let's go tonight.' Only my father said nothing.

'The weather's perfect at the moment,' said my wife, 'and it would be fun for the kids, too.'

It seemed a lunatic scheme to me. Ten camp beds with bedding; six adults and four children with food for a couple of days all to be packed into two cars at a few hours notice. Where were we to get the camp beds from – we had only three of our own? We did get them, however. The whole family fanned out around our village like troops foraging for an army and by late afternoon the problem was solved. By nightfall the cars were packed and ready to move off. We all tried, without success, to snatch a few hours sleep and by three o'clock we were struggling into whatever spaces were left between the food and luggage, and the engines were started up.

It was a fine night, certainly, as we drove westward and we were well on our way along almost empty roads by the time the sun came up behind us. It sent bright fingers of light through the back windows and flashed promise of a golden day from the rear-view mirrors. My brother's car, packed like a telephone kiosk at a students' rag, hummed along behind us. I was beginning to warm to the whole thing myself. In a few short hours we would be there and I could watch everyone's faces as they took it all in. The mill in summer – what a prospect. How they would envy me as they wandered about the paddocks laced with dancing streams and set against a perfect backdrop of rolling hills. When they saw the rugged symmetry of the buildings, felt the quiet serenity of the atmosphere and heard the sound of running water against the very walls – what would they say?

I began to feel like a criminal. There have never been too many water-mills about and with little prospect of any more being built in the future, it seemed greedy somehow to have one of my own. Perhaps I'd been too boastful about it. Perhaps I should play it down a bit when we got there.

We were well into Cornwall when the rain began to fall. Within minutes the windscreen wipers were struggling to cope as the rain enveloped us like a tidal wave. I could no longer see my brother's car behind. I could only dimly discern the road ahead. We were into the narrow lanes by now, hemmed in on either side and with sheets of water pouring towards us down steep slopes. In ten minutes I knew that we were lost and almost panicked when I remembered the GPO van we met on our earlier journey through these lanes.

'I hope we don't meet the postman,' I said. My wife is not a Catholic but she crossed herself.

'Be quiet and watch where you're going,' she moaned. 'You'll frighten the children.'

'What did the postman do?' enquired my daughter, leaning forward to make herself heard above the thundering metal roof.

'Can I have a sandwich?'

'Isn't that the ivy-covered chimney of the old mine we have to pass?' Rhona enquired, peering through the almost opaque side window. A dim silhouette suggested that she was right and a glimmer of hope sustained me as we pressed on into the deluge. I was hoping to recognize a cottage with a wrought iron lantern on its white gable end where I should turn left. We went on for several miles before I swung round near a cottage which looked vaguely like the one we wanted. In another ten miles we had settled into quiet despair.

'Where's Uncle Alan?' asked the children, scrubbing away at the film of condensation on the back window. 'We can't see any car behind. Does he know the way to the mill, Dad? Does he, Dad? Can we have a sandwich? Why aren't we there yet, Dad?'

'Look,' said my wife. 'There's the old mine shaft again.' It was the same dim shape we had seen twenty minutes before. I pulled the car into the road side and covered my face. In seconds the windows were blanked out by condensation.

'Why have we stopped, Dad? There's a car trying to get past us, Dad.' It drew alongside and stopped.

'Ask them where we are,' said my wife as I wound my window down. My sister-in-law was peering through the rain from the other car, my brother's face stared blankly over her shoulder.

'Where have you been?' I asked, with commendable presence of mind.

'We got lost,' shouted Kath. 'It was ages ago. We've been round half of Cornwall looking for you.'

'Never mind,' I said. 'We're not far away now. I'll go ahead slowly – try to keep up.' I shut the window and moved off. We must have turned at the right cottage this time for we eventually found ourselves in the whitewashed village with the river bridge and pub. Alan's car was no more than two feet behind ours as we eased round the corner on to the steep slope down the valley side to the mill.

The rain was still sheeting down as we came to a halt in the yard and the brakes of my brother's car squeaked as he drew up behind us. The mill was a grey shape behind the curtain of rain. Cascades of water poured from sagging gutters and broken downspouts and splashed into a miniature lake which stretched across the yard. The old front door still lay on its side against the wall and heaps of

broken slates and plaster emerged from the iron-grey water, like rocky islands in a turgid sea.

We sat for long moments, a silent core in the thundering metal, overwhelmed, like the pounding windscreen wipers, by the sheer volume of water. Then, with plastic macs over our heads, we exploded from the cars in twos and threes, splashing and leaping for the shelter of the front entrance like demented bats eager for the safety of a belfry. Impelled by the stinging rain, we jammed the doorway and shot through into the dim interior. An eerie feeling crept over us as our feet made no sound. The flooring had been ripped up and flung outside and we padded about on dark earth. The flowered wallpaper had gone and the plaster was hacked from the stone walls. Strange pipes emerged from gaping holes like beckoning fingers and the fireplace was a black void where the range had once been.

A new bath, its virgin whiteness marred only by the dark scrape marks of some workman's hob-nail boots, lay in the centre of the floor, accentuating the air of desolation. We moved, mute and silent-footed, from room to room like mourners at a funeral and found no comfort. Only the hissing of the rain disturbed the stillness. In the scullery I unbolted the back door to show them the valley but had to slam it shut to avoid the flood. I went upstairs, followed by the more adventurous souls among us. We mounted slowly, clutching the handrail and testing each step like mountaineers traversing the steep face of a glacier. Our last hopes of comfort were snuffed out as we sidled along the bedroom walls, peering down gaping holes where rotten floorboards had been torn out and we watched with fascination as shining rivulets of water coursed down the damp walls in search of any sound timber still holding out. We returned as quickly as we dared to rejoin the rest of the party below and stood in a dejected circle waiting for someone to speak. 'No house looks its best in the rain,' said Alan, without looking at me. I had made several attempts to say something myself since we left the cars but nothing would come. I noticed my father looking at me with a bewildered expression, as if he were unable to believe what his eyes told him. 'Give it a year, Dad,' I croaked. He looked nervously up at the sagging ceiling.

'I'll give it a year,' he replied, as if he doubted that the structure would stand up that long.

'Wait until you see the mill,' I said, and wished I hadn't. We splashed across the angle of the yard into the interior which I had so lovingly described to them all. It was darker than I expected and there was more rubbish lying about than I remembered. We huddled in the doorway and peered into the gloom. The swollen millrace roared against the wall and the pulleys, hoppers and great toothed wheels loomed in the shadows like instruments of torture in some satanic dungeon. A nameless metal object clanked monotonously in the workings and the whole edifice trembled and creaked. 'Isn't it magnificent?' I shouted above the din, but nobody heard. My voice was carried away in the crashing waters but it didn't matter. The whole family was back in the cottage sitting round the edge of the bath. 'The trout in that millstream must be getting a move on,' said my father as I rejoined them.

Half an hour later we were having a welcome meal in the most comfortable place we could find; we ate our sandwiches perched round the granite base of the cider-press like tits round a peanut feeder. It was dry in there and there were things to sit on. We had become immune to the sound of the rain which had not ceased for an instant since it started. By chance it was my brother's birthday and Rhona produced a cake which she had iced as a surprise. She had brought a large household candle, too, to light us to our camp beds and she stuck it on top of the cake and lit it. We all sang 'Happy birthday to you'.

The rain still had not slackened as we crammed everything back into the cars. 'Would anyone like to see the river before we go?' I offered.

'We've seen it,' said my father. 'I've got half of it in my shoes.'

They were all wedged tightly in the cars waiting to go. The rain finally stopped somewhere on the long road home but I can't remember where. We were all safely in our beds by one o'clock the next morning.

'There's a letter for you,' said my wife when I next opened my eyes about nine hours later. It was from the insurance company asking if I would kindly send them a cheque to cover fire risk at the mill.

Trouble at t'Mill

One thing that Mr Pretty did with surprising efficiency was to send me a key to the gate. Penruin was wide open in every sense of the word and there were many objects lying about, both inside and outside the buildings, which I was anxious to preserve. Many pieces of machinery had been scattered about in the yard, the orchard and even in the fields. I was not sure what they were but I was anxious that they should not be lost before I was in a position to find out. I had, therefore, asked the builder to rescue the tubular metal gate which was lying in the nettles and cowparsley in the orchard and fit it back between the stone posts near the top of the lane. He was to fasten it securely with a padlock and send a key to me, give one to Surgey, so that he could take his animals in and out, and keep another for himself.

I received my key in June, taped inside a note which assured me that all was now secure but Don Chambers reported that he had seen no gate on subsequent visits, nor had we seen one on my brother's birthday in August. There was still no gate across the lane when Don and I visited the mill in December in spite of endless reminders from us both, which were sidestepped with bewildering dexterity. It was a cold wet journey that December day and we arrived in the gloom of mid-afternoon.

The cottage seemed deserted and desolate until we opened the door of the sittingroom which had been tight shut. Three local artisans were sitting in semi-darkness upon bags of cement and staring at us as if we were visitors from Mars. They tried to push playing cards into their pockets with varying success and mumbled that they were waiting for Mr Pretty to pick them up in his van. They had been engaged in painting, they said, pointing to a collection of tins in a dark corner. The inside of the door was still wet with white paint which had run in long rivulets down its surface and coagulated here and there into sticky blobs. Some streams had

reached the bottom and dripped off on to the floor.

We were aghast at the sight. It was like looking at a small waterfall which had suddenly frozen solid. Although the plaster work was not finished in any room there were other isolated doors and window-frames treated in a similar manner. When we returned to the sittingroom the workmen had gone. No vehicle of any kind had approached the mill to pick them up; they had simply vanished into the encroaching darkness.

A recent letter had informed us that the septic tank drainage system had been completed and water was now laid on. We had had a lot of trouble with the water. The local analyst had reported that our crystal spring in the orchard was polluted and suggested that the swarming population in his test-tube was due to the presence of cattle in the field above (that gentle face with big, liquid eyes which had watched us over the hedge that April morning). Mr Pretty calmed our panic at this devastating discovery and assured us that it could easily be overcome. He would build a concrete tank around the spring which would isolate it from all contamination. He had completed this job in September and sent us another analyst's report which declared the water now safe for human consumption. The tank was, in reality, a new concrete sewer pipe sunk vertically into the ground to enclose the spring. A black polythene tube carried water from this protective sheath, beneath the orchard, to a storage tank on the grinding floor of the mill.

When I first inspected the completed system in October I had found a dead bird floating inside the concrete pipe. The builder pointed out that it was not easy to find a stone slab large enough to cover the top but that, after endless trouble and expense, he had, by great good fortune, located one at last which he had planned to put over the spring the very next day. I insisted on another analyst's report before the spring was sealed and all now seemed to be well at last. Don had been next to visit Penruin. He reported that when he had turned on the tap in the scullery there had been a cacophony of noise and, after an interval, a stream of thick black liquid had oozed into his glass with a yellowish head upon it that any Guinness drinker might envy.

Mr Pretty was baffled at first but soon located the trouble. His plumber, he explained, had connected the cottage by mistake to an old water pipe he had uncovered outside the wall of the mill and, in so doing, had bypassed our newly installed system altogether. What had emerged from the tap had come from some other source entirely, but he evaded our questions on this matter as skilfully as our repeated enquiries about the gate. As he pointed out, it was not a major problem. The cottage was reconnected to the supply from the spring. But his plumber forgot to reinter the pipe he had uncovered and it froze solid during that winter, cutting off the water supply to half the cottages and farms in the area. At the time of our visit in December all had been reported well and ready for our use. By the time we had grumbled our way around the cottage it was too dark to inspect the septic tank drainage system outside, so we decided to have a cup of tea and a sandwich and pay a visit to Mr Pretty at Pollen to express our dissatisfaction with his work to date.

When we tried to fill our kettle there was no noise this time, nor was there any water, dirty or otherwise.

We were without both tea and patience by the time we confronted him in his front parlour. We felt that the crunch had come at last. This time he would have to be told that the standard of work was not good enough and that unless there was a drastic change in both speed and quality of effort we would be forced to seek alternative service. Don keyed himself up to deliver his ultimatum in his best professional manner. 'There is no water supply at the mill, Mr Pretty,' he said. 'It really is not good enough. The electric pump does not work and unless . . .'

'Did you prime it, midear?' said Mr Pretty, settling into an armchair and stuffing a bundle of tobacco into his pipe.

'Prime it?' said Don. 'Prime what?'

The builder applied a match to the loose tobacco and puffed with such energy that we all disappeared in a cloud of smoke whilst smouldering threads fell on to his shirt front, his trouser legs and down the sides of the chair cushions. Some sparks shot upwards until they went out like spent rockets at a firework display.

'Did you prime the pump first?' repeated Mr Pretty, thrashing at the offending sparks.

'We didn't know it had to be primed,' said Don, somewhat deflated. The builder cackled with laughter as if Don had said he didn't know he had to tie his shoelaces.

'You'm got to prime it, midear soul,' he chortled. 'Else you'll have an air lock in the pipe if you only draw water once in a blue moon.'

He went on to explain the technical details with maddening patience. There was, it seemed, a metal pipe sticking up in the middle of the orchard which was connected beneath the ground to the plastic pipe which carried the water from the spring. The polythene pipe sloped gently down from this point in both directions so that if there was any loss of water through leakage or evaporation, an air bubble would be formed at that point and no other. It was a simple matter, therefore, to eliminate an airlock by unscrewing the cap on the metal standpipe and pouring in water until it came to the top of the tube. The electric pump in the mill would then be able to go into action and draw the supply from the spring up into the storage tank. There was no denying the sense and logic of what he said. His amusement at our ignorance of the finer points of priming pumps rather blunted the edge of our determination to bring him to heel.

Don countered by switching his frontal attack to a more oblique angle. 'We've been having a look at the work done at Penruin, Mr Pretty,' he said, surveying the room in which we were sitting, 'and to tell the truth, we're baffled.' He looked at the plaster alsatian which stood on a table in the window, at the green and red gnome fishing into the goldfish bowl on the piano and at the pale pink doors. 'You're obviously a man of taste,' he said. 'I can see at a glance that you like to have everything just so in your own house, and yet you allow the standard of workmanship at the mill to be far below what you yourself consider necessary in a comfortable home. I'm afraid,' he went on, 'that the decoration, such as it is, has been carried out by unskilled labourers and is not acceptable. All work must be done by professional tradesmen exactly as detailed in my specification.' Mr Pretty seemed about to protest but Don pressed

on with his attack. 'I have inspected the sittingroom door which has been painted today. Not only is it a mess, but the paint has been applied without proper preparation and without even an under-coat.'

The builder's resistance seemed to falter a little at this point and he promised that he would meet us at the mill the following morning without fail and go over every detail with us. If anything was below standard, he assured us, it would be made good and in any case he would like to make sure that we were able to prime the pump properly. He would also like to show us the septic tank drainage, which had gone without a hitch.

The mill cottage had been so depressing that we had planned to find some comfort and refreshment at a pub after we had confronted the builder. We asked him if he could recommend such a hostelry. If we took the road out of the village to the north-east, he said, we would come to the Two Ravens. It was only a few miles distant and we could not miss it. It was a pitch-black night outside and raining hard and, although we were dressed for rough weather, we were fairly wet by the time we had scrambled into the car. Whenever I try to visualize a black hole in outer space I think of that terrible drive. The only things we could see clearly were shining rods of rain slanting into the inadequate headlights like steel arrows. We were on the open moors where even the comparative comfort of walls and hedges had disappeared and the road surface was almost invisible. We sat hunched forward with our faces pressed almost to the windscreen as the car seemed to climb endlessly into the buffeting wind and lashing rain. After what seemed like an hour we had given up hope of locating the pub and were praying fervently that we would not run off the road into some bottomless bog. We glimpsed only a few rocky outcrops to right and left and the red eyes of a saturated bullock as we brushed past his humped form in the corridor of wild darkness. Even the mill cottage seemed to us then like some distant Shangri-la.

At length we saw a tiny light ahead, a steady spark in the whirling elements and a glimmer of hope in our despair. It was the lighted window of an isolated house. As I got out of the car to seek help my hat blew off in the darkness and I trod it underfoot in the mud. I crammed it back on my head and felt the water trickle down my face as I fumbled for the latch of the front gate. The sound and flicker of a television set came from beyond the red curtain of light as I knocked on the door. A dog barked and crashed against the door and there was a scuffle and muffled shouts within as someone tried to get it under control. A man opened the door, leaning heavily backwards in an effort to hold a slavering hound as big as a great dane.

'You're on the wrong road for the Ravens,' he shouted when I had made my enquiry between the deep throated bayings. 'You'll have to turn round if you've come from Pollen direction and go back for about three miles . . . Down! Sultan. Down boy! . . . There's a turning to the left . . . Shut your noise . . . Enid! . . . Give me a hand with this damned dog.' I was several paces down the path ready to run as the man and his wife dragged the dog away. I was still standing in the pelting rain when he returned to the door. 'Go back to Three Lanes,' he panted, 'and take the left turn. The Ravens is about two miles on.'

I thanked him and turned into sudden blackness as he slammed the door. I almost crashed into Don in the middle of the road. 'What the hell happened?' he asked. 'I thought you were being eaten.'

'Get in the car quick,' I shouted. 'I've just met the Baskervilles.' I tried to turn the car in the narrow lane but as I reversed for the third time the rear wheels started to spin on the muddy verge and Don had to get out to push. With one leg in a ditch he managed to persuade the car back on to the road surface. He climbed back in, covered with mud and water. His trousers were so wet that he rolled the legs up to his knees and emptied a shoe out of the window.

The sight of the whitewashed pub, in its pool of light, revived our spirits a little and the thought of a drink at last in the warm bar with a log fire, perhaps, and even a little supper made us almost cheerful as we pushed open the door. The room was brightly lit and covered with patterned carpet which ran on up the front of the Spanish-style bar at the far end. A number of couples dressed for an evening out were perched on chromium and leather bar stools, sipping pink and green liquids from tiny glasses. A one-bar electric fire with wrought tin decorations and paper coal cast imitation flames on its

reflector. The occupants stared at us as if we were shipwrecked sailors who had just crawled out of the sea. Don had slipped his shoe back on but had forgotten to roll down his trouser legs. He adjusted his dress while I ordered two pints of beer and smokey bacon crisps. The night-outers seemed stunned into silence as the barman in neat grey suit and neat grey moustache served me without comment. We retired to a small wrought table near the door and, although a little muted conversation had broken out again at the bar, every crunch of our crisps crackled round the room.

We caught sight of ourselves in a wall mirror, shaped like a butterfly. I had removed my hat but it had left a dark line of mud around my forehead so that I looked like a Cree Indian who had lost his feather. 'Hellfire,' said Don. 'They think we're convicts on the run.' We stuffed the rest of our crisps into our pockets and went out. It was a relief to be back in the rain. We managed to get back to the mill eventually, dried out as well as we could and slid into the luxury of our damp sleeping bags. 'It's a judgement on me,' wailed Don. 'I've been forced to spend half my life converting real pubs into dumps like that.'

We awoke early the next morning and wanted only one thing from life – a steaming hot mug of tea. It was a relief to find the sun was shining and the air had turned mild, almost balmy. The nightmare of the previous evening seemed like a knockabout comedy to us then, as we walked across the orchard with a plastic bucket and collected water from the spring to prime the pump. We had no difficulty in locating the standpipe but it was sealed at the top with a large nut which we could not move. We were still unshaven and in our pyjama jackets as we rummaged through the car boot, looking for a suitable spanner. When we eventually removed the nut Don sent me up to the millstone floor to watch what was happening in the tank and to shout reports to him through the half door, while he squatted in the middle of the orchard with the bucket. Nothing happened when the pipe was filled up and the nut replaced, but after I had kicked the tank a few times the pump suddenly sprang into action and the water started to flow. We were leaping about, cheering in the orchard, when Mr Pretty arrived.

By the time we had gone over all the outstanding problems inside the cottage and were walking outside to inspect the septic tank, we felt we were making real progress at last. There was a pile of rocks like a prehistoric burial mound near the wall of the kitchen garden. It looked as if it weighed about twenty tons. Nothing else was visible. 'Where is the drainage system?' asked Don.

'There,' said Mr Pretty, indicating the rock-pile with his pipe stem.

'You mean its underneath all that?' queried Don, his face screwed up in disbelief.

'Well, I know'd you gents like everything neat an' tidy,' said the builder, 'you wouldn't 'ave wanted all that spoil scattered about the place so I cleared it up for you.'

'Where's the inspection cover, then?' insisted Don. 'I can't look at the tanks without an inspection cover.'

'It's there,' said Mr Pretty looking a little hurt. 'Course, if you want to put your 'ed in, I'll 'ave the rocks shifted, midear.' Whilst Don was trying to think of something to say the builder fumbled inside his coat and pulled out a turnip watch. 'Is that the time?' he squeaked, 'I'll 'ave to be off. I've got a funeral this morning – interment in 'arf an hour.' He hurried away with the brim of his bowler hat trembling over his ears. 'If you want the sewer exhumed let me know,' he called as he disappeared round the corner of the cowshed.

Don picked up a handful of stones and flung them viciously at the rock-pile. 'If we can't beat 'em,' he shouted, 'we might as well bloody join 'em.'

Water, Water Everywhere

It was water that attracted me to Penruin in the first place, so I suppose that I could not really grumble when I got it. The rocks which covered the drains were a blessing in the weeks that followed because the septic tank was out of sight and, consequently, more or less out of mind. We never did find out what was really beneath the burial mound. It could have been a dead horse for all we knew but, apart from a few twinges when I paid the bill, we didn't worry too much about it and we certainly had no trouble from water once it left the cottage. Water coming in, however, was a different matter.

It came down the chimneys in alarming quantities and sometimes, if the wind was in the wrong direction, under the doors. The yard turned into a small lake after heavy rain, which was frequent, and sometimes lapped against the cottage wall. I cured this particular trouble by hammering a metal rod between the stones of the yard until it reached the tail-race culvert below. I had a much harder job getting it out again but it was worth the trouble. Whenever the yard threatened to flood I had only to clear the drain-hole with a long cane and the water would run away into the stream below. The water supply from the spring was always a bit erratic and we could never be certain that the electric pump would work. When we turned on the taps we would sometimes get a smooth supply but often there would be a long interval and then a high pressure jet would explode into the bowl and wet us from head to toe. During the daylight hours it did not bother us over much but at night, when all the world was still and every tiny sound was magnified, we could hear the whole system churning and groaning and gurgling with all the horror of an upset stomach.

We became hypersensitive to the pipes, the cistern, the pump and even the distant spring and we worried about them all like hypochondriacs. When we had flushed the lavatory in the bathroom we would leap into bed and sit rigid, listening to the long-drawn-out sequence of noises that followed. The cistern would fill up slowly with a slurp-slurping sound and the relatively large volume of water which it drew from the mill tank would usually lower the level to the point where the trip-switch was thrown and the electric pump would go into action. It would whine and labour as it sucked the water through the polythene pipe and squirted it into the tank until the level was high enough to shut it off again. It was impossible to relax, much less to compose one's self to sleep, until we had listened to the whole painful rigmarole in its correct order and been reasonably convinced by ultimate silence that all was loaded, cocked and ready to go again if anyone else was inconsiderate enough to use the bathroom again.

Even when we went to bed comparatively fresh, we were exhausted by the time it was all over. The real worries started, however, when the electric pump failed to function after a large volume of water had been drawn off. It could mean a number of things; it could mean that not quite enough had been used to trip the switch, in which case one was forced to get out of bed to run some more off to make sure that was, in fact, what had happened. On the other hand it could mean that something awful had got into the tank and jammed up the levers or that there was an air lock in the middle of the orchard which would have to be attended to before any more water could be used. It was possible, too, that the electric pump had developed a fault and might at that very moment be getting hot so that it would burst into flames when we were all asleep and turn the whole place into a raging inferno.

We were freed from these nocturnal worries suddenly in the summer. The orchard spring dried up. We had to carry water from the mill leat and boil it. Mr Pretty said that the disgusting brew, which had issued from the tap when it was connected by mistake to the underground pipe by the mill, was due to the pipe being unused for many years. If it was properly flushed out, he said, it would be quite clean so he went ahead and flushed it, and it was. We were not too sure where the water came from, however, so we boiled all our drinking water in the dry season and went back to our spring when it sprang again.

The hot water tank in the airing cupboard had been fitted with an immersion heater but, contrary to Don's instructions, it did not have a thermostat, so that from time to time it would frighten us out of our wits by boiling violently. It was safe enough because it had an overflow pipe which carried the steam and boiling water back to the storage tank in the mill. At our urgent request the builder had fitted a cover on the tank to keep out dust and other undesirable things but, unfortunately, he omitted to take the overflow pipe into consideration and fitted the cover below the outlet. The next time the water over-heated we were stunned to see steam rising from the eaves and hot water running out of the door of the mill.

The open fireplaces looked very attractive when they were restored to their original state but the removal of the Victorian grate and range restored them also to the big open passageways to the sky, which they must have been when they were first built. Their effect on the temperature inside the cottage was much the same as leaving all the doors open. As far as rain was concerned it was even worse. A man could have climbed straight up them with an average door on his back and if it was raining at the time he would most likely have been washed down again like a spider from a drainpipe. In a heavy downpour the bigger fireplace in the livingroom looked like an indoor shower with the water turned on.

It was a bit of a disappointment, to be honest, because I felt it would be more sensible to install a grid in the fireplace rather than the wrought-iron basket which I had envisaged. To counter the problem I had large flat stones put over each chimney and raised on bricks to about six inches above the opening so that smoke could escape freely all round. I was very pleased with the result. It looked very good from the outside and reduced the indoor rainstorms to a fine drizzle.

I am not sure whether this arrangement precipitated the next development by making the chimneys more inviting or whether it would have happened anyway. The fact is that the jackdaws were attracted to those chimneys like wasps to a jampot. One could now sit before the fireplace and watch twigs (and often quite big sticks) falling where rain drops fell before. Once, when we had been absent from the place for several weeks, we found the entire fireplace full of twigs which were piled so high that they disappeared up the chimney. We filled a tea chest up and emptied it outside six times before the fireplace was properly clear.

I had been so preoccupied with the buildings at Penruin that I had not had time to spend a day fishing in the river and had been

looking forward to doing so ever since Rhona and I had picnicked on its banks the day we discovered the mill. None of my angling friends had been down to Cornwall at that time, nor had my painting companions, and I was anxious to get to know the river a little before they joined me there. The water which fed the mill leat came from the river at a point about a quarter of a mile away. A large, deep pool had been created there by a smooth concrete ledge along the top of a line of natural rocks so that it formed a dam across the width of the river. There was an escape channel on the far bank to carry away excess water when the river was in spate, but even when the water was low the dam held back sufficient water to maintain a constant supply to the mill-stream through a heavy iron grating designed to keep the leat free from driftwood and other flotsam brought down by flood water.

After tumbling over the edge of the dam the river ran on through a series of delightful little canyons, rich with ferns and mosses and overhung here and there by tall trees whose leaves cast a mystical green light upon the shining pools. The sunlit canopy seemed to throw back a subtle echo in those rocky grottos, varying the music of the running water. Rhona was busy hanging curtains in the cottage and I took the opportunity to explore the river so that I could learn the safest and most interesting line to take when wading the water with my trout rod, for I had decided to get up early the next morning and fish for the first time. There were sea-trout deep down in the mill pool; I could see them clearly, lying like flotillas of small submarines on the sandy flats between the rocks. There were many brown trout, too, in the foaming runnels and shallower basins and, although they all seemed to be very small, there was promise of better game where the water ran deep between the great boulders. There were exciting secret places, too, under the steep banks and beneath the convoluted rocks where the wilier, and perhaps much bigger, trout seemed likely to be lying. Perhaps even a salmon or two might be waiting there to move up stream when they felt the next flood of fresh cold water from the hills. It was the sort of place where one might wander all day long, forgetting time and the rush and worry of the outside world, for it was a complete, though miniature, world of its own. Its inhabitants had lived out their lives there free, for the most part, of man's disturbing influence for ten thousand years and more. The herons had stalked the pools with cautious, wary paces and the dippers, bowing like courteous little gentlemen in evening dress upon the wet boulders, had explored every watery crevice and smooth runnel for their food through countless ages.

All the inhabitants of that little world depended on the natural growing things which surrounded them and upon each other for their continued existence. Nature had ordained that they should hunt to live and I was entitled, as a fellow creature, to hunt the fish if I wanted them for food, but not to destroy them, nor any part of the world that they and I live in, for personal greed or perverted gratification.

The curtains were hung in the livingroom when I returned to the cottage and it was beginning to look like home at last. I prepared my fishing tackle for an early start the next morning and Rhona put away her materials and made the supper. As it grew dark it became quite chilly and, although we had no fuel prepared, a cheerful blaze seemed very desirable. There were some old wooden boxes, a

broken tea chest and some other rubbish in the cowshed which I had not yet cleared out, so I took a torch and returned with all the combustible material I could find and parked it in the hearth.

We bolted the doors, pulled up our chairs and prepared to eat supper by our first fire. Bright flames soon licked up the pyramid of fuel, casting warm light upon the walls and flickering upon the china plates we had hung there. Thick black smoke began to curl away up the wide chimney and then curled down again. It billowed into the room and enveloped us in a foul cloud of darkness. We sprang from our chairs, beating at it with our arms, but it had hardly thinned out at all when the next black wave came rolling out, followed by another and another. We scrambled to the door alternately coughing and trying to hold our breath. By the time we had unbolted the door and run outside we had almost choked to death. It had started to rain and we had to stay out there for a long time before we could enter the cottage again to open the windows and doors. It was late by the time the fire was out and the air was clear enough to breathe freely. We were wet and very cold. Our first fire had been lit and we were almost frozen by it.

We were awakened during the night by the rattle of rain as it beat against the bedroom windows and howled in the gusting wind about the chimneys. The heavens were split apart by writhing branches of lightning, a kaleidoscope of ever-changing patterns like inverted trees, etched in bright silver upon the black night. The room was lit like daytime by flashes of pallid blue light and the thunder rolled and crashed and echoed back and forth across the world. The rain closed in upon the cottage like a hissing monster until the roof and walls became a diving bell protecting us from watery suffocation. The next morning the rain had stopped and I looked out upon the river field where little groups of sheep stood marooned on small hillocks, dark against the shining sheets of water

which surrounded them. I put on my thigh waders, gathered up my fishing tackle and splashed across the sodden ground to the river where I was staggered by the transformation. The banks had been about five to six feet above the water level when I walked along it the evening before but now the river was a raging torrent, tearing its way between the bordering trees and spilling over as brown as army tea into the meadows on either side. Tree branches as heavy as a man could lift and dark rafts of tangled vegetation went spinning

by, sinking below the turgid surface and reappearing again downstream, twisting, turning and sinking again under the powerful muscles of the brawny river. From time to time great baulks of timber would rise from the flood like the black necks of water monsters, their lower ends caught and held for moments by the rocks below. They would swing up high into the air and crash over as they were torn out by the fierce current and carried away on the flood. Here and there heavy branches had been trapped by the exposed roots of trees along the bank and jammed tight by the force of the relentless water which foamed white and angry against the black timber. The river had cast sodden clumps of debris around them and flotsam streamed from the tangled twigs like tresses of dark hair in the wind.

It is difficult to imagine that this was the same little river that whispered such beguiling music only yesterday. I looked in vain for the melancholy heron and the dipper. A grey wagtail was doing his dance routine by a small pool of floodwater in the river field and a carrion crow, hunched like a sinister undertaker on a branch, surveyed the turbulent flood for any drowned corpse which he might turn to his account. It was not easy to visualize the tiny trout coping with the devastating deluge which was raging over them. They were safe enough from any poor efforts of mine to catch them until the flood subsided but it must have been a savage world down there with stones and debris hurtling about them in the speeding water. No man in his right senses, however strong, would have dared to enter the river in its present anger. Yet the trout could use their ounce and less of strength to ride out the storm under the protection of a boulder or a ledge of rock, for they were always there on station as if nothing untoward had happened when the water cleared and settled back to normal flow again.

I could see no sea-trout now in the mill pool, which had coloured like coffee and was pouring a foot deep over the lip of the dam. It crashed and foamed upon the rocks below, sending up a drifting mist of spray like a miniature Niagara. The bypass stream bulged like a glossy, well-fed serpent, full to the brim with racing water. The grating at the millrace entrance was bristling with shattered twigs and branches packed tight against its iron bars by the pressing water. But I made no attempt to clear it, for I had no desire to risk my neck on the slippery rocks beside the torrent. In any case, the blockage turned the metal grid into an almost solid barrier against the high water which would have swamped the leat and, no doubt, have caused some damage to its shallow banks. Already the little stream was spilling over all along its length. The sluice gate at the mill was almost derelict but still it held back most of the extra flow and forced it to escape down the sloping hillside to the river.

I saw no other living soul that day in the little valley which was coping with the flood alone as it had always done throughout the ages. One would not have guessed that humans lived there, or had ever lived, had it not been for the bottle and white plastic container that spun together in the flotsam of a small protected bay.

I had planned to widen the mill leat later when more urgent matters were attended to, and form a trout pool in the meadow. The local river authority were very helpful and promised to assist me with their guidance when the time came. Two members of the board took time and trouble to visit me and discuss my plans. They told me too about their efforts to count the salmon moving up the river to spawn in the narrow gravel streamlets of the high country, and told me how best to build groynes or croys against the river bank to form small areas of protected water where salmon would be encouraged to lie. They frightened me, however, by suggesting that if I built my trout pool I might have to pay for water on a gallonage basis.

When I returned from the river that day of the flood I stood by the scullery door and looked again across the valley. At a penny per gallon I would have had to be a multi-millionaire to pay for half of it.

The Country Life

Mr Pretty's resistance to hanging the gate finally crumbled. It was restored to its hinges between the granite posts and secured with a padlock and chain. It was gratifying to be able to use my key at last and to know that Surgey and the builder were using theirs, because I had paid for them long ago and anyway it was nice to feel that Penruin was now secure when we were not there.

We had not seen Surgey for some time but it was obvious that he was making good use of the grazing because there were often bullocks or sheep in the fields. When sheep were there all would be comparatively peaceful except for their irritating habit of rolling on to their backs in the shallow hollows, so that they could not get up again. No-one from the farm seemed to notice their plight. I knew that sheep did silly things like that and that if they were left without assistance they might eventually die, but I thought the phenomenon was rare. Not so with Surgey's sheep. They seemed to regard it as normal behaviour. It became a regular chore for me to go out with a broom and roll a few the right way up before breakfast. I sometimes wondered how the Australians dealt with the problem on their vast sheep farms in the Outback. If their merinos were anything like the Cornish sheep it must be a fulltime occupation keeping them on their feet.

Like most sheep, they were inoffensive creatures, however, except for a ram that appeared on my premises from time to time, hung about with a variety of hardware. The first time I saw him he had a triangle of wooden planks round his neck as if he had burst out of a shed and brought half the wall with him. I found the gap in the hedge where he had forced himself and his timber collar through the tangled vegetation and I kept at a respectful distance. I was glad to find he had gone the next morning, leaving only another gap at the top of the bank, but I saw him in my field a few weeks later wearing a metal disc the size of a dustbin lid. On another occasion he was trundling a baulk of timber as big as a gatepost, which was attached to his back legs by a rope. I learned later that he belonged to a farmer, a few miles down the valley, who had fixed almost every object on his farm to the ram at one time or another but without much success. The ram's romantic wanderings were hardly affected and he was known far and wide in the valley as Houdini.

The bullocks were a different matter. They were wild, unruly creatures. We met a group of them in the lane once and I was foolish enough to try driving slowly towards them in the hope that they would move out of the way. They ignored us completely and started a head-to-head trial of strength with each other, pushing and scrimaging like kids in a school playground. One of them backed into us suddenly and crumpled the nearside wing like a paper bag before I could get the car into reverse.

We arrived one day to find a large section of the orchard wall had been knocked down. I suspected that Surgey's cattle were responsible. He denied it vigorously and said that the damage had been caused by a herd which belonged to Dan Mather, a more-or-less nomadic character who frequented the moors and was as wild and lawless as his cattle. It was Dan's habit, Surgey said, to slip a

bunch of steers into any field he found unoccupied and claim that they had got in without his knowledge or approval.

It had taken a lot of time and much frustration before the gate at Penruin had been put in place, and it puzzled me how herds of cattle could pass freely in and out if it were kept locked. Surgey swore that he had never left it unsecured and said that he had reported the activities of Dan Mather to Constable Martin from Trellic. I went to see the policeman a few days later at his cottage in Trellic village. He said that he had not clapped eyes on Surgey for two or three years and that poor old Dan was used as a scapegoat for every misdemeanour that occurred in the locality. 'He's probably telling the truth, mind, when he says he's never left your gate unlocked, sir,' he added. 'I've seen Mr Pretty going in and out with his vehicles several times when I've been cycling that way and *he* never uses any key.'

'How does he get in then?' I asked.

'Oh, he just lifts the gate off its hinges and swings it back the other way, sir,' he said. 'They're not daft down here, you know.'

We were rather pleased with the new bathroom when it was finished. For some strange reason it attracted a buzzard. I don't know what his game was but he would sit on the half door of the mill and stare at me through the window when I was shaving. I am fond of birds and buzzards are handsome creatures so that, at first, I felt like St Francis of Assisi. But hawks of any kind can give you a nasty stare over that great hooked beak and after a few days he began to

make me uneasy. I stopped waving to him and tried ignoring him altogether, but it's difficult to concentrate on shaving when a hawk is staring at you. I found myself descending to verbal abuse, but it had no effect. I had never seen a wild hawk so close before outside a zoo, certainly not a hawk that was interested in me.

Now I had never had an interesting idea in my life whilst shaving in spite of the popularly-held belief that brilliant notions are common at such times; in fact, my mind is usually a complete blank until eleven a.m. But it came to me suddenly that if this bird was going to pose in front of me every morning as if he were stuffed, I might be able to make an astonishingly detailed and accurate drawing of him. The next morning I was ready and I had whipped out a sketchbook and pencil in seconds. I studied him closely and with the greatest care. His eyes were magnificent orbs of smooth crystal with deep jet-black pupils, circled with rings of glowing amber. I could see a minute reflection of the cottage wall and window on the glassy surface. My pencil had hardly touched the paper when he flew away. I never saw him again. Human beings often show the same reaction when I start to draw them. I wonder if it's the way I stare at them that makes them so uneasy.

I had another odd experience in the bathroom. When the decoration was complete I decided to plug the wall so that I could fit a towel rail by the washbasin. I'd had considerable experience of what can happen when one starts to hammer holes in old plaster, so I took the utmost care. The first three holes were made and plugged without much trouble but, as everyone knows, it is the last hole that usually triggers off disaster, so I was even more circumspect when I used the hammer. My worst fears were realized when I found the plaster hard and unyielding and I knew that I would have to give the punch a lusty blow. I gave it three good clouts and then three more, and was astonished and relieved to find the wall showed no signs of collapse and disintegration. I was just reaching over to pick the last rawlplug out of the bath when a piece of plaster as big as a dinnerplate fell out of the ceiling and shattered all over my back.

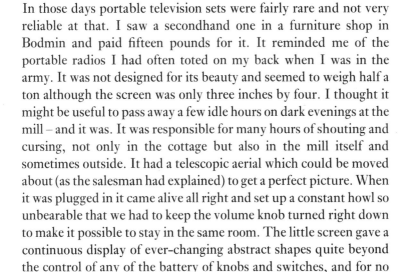

In those days portable television sets were fairly rare and not very reliable at that. I saw a secondhand one in a furniture shop in Bodmin and paid fifteen pounds for it. It reminded me of the portable radios I had often toted on my back when I was in the army. It was not designed for its beauty and seemed to weigh half a ton although the screen was only three inches by four. I thought it might be useful to pass away a few idle hours on dark evenings at the mill – and it was. It was responsible for many hours of shouting and cursing, not only in the cottage but also in the mill itself and sometimes outside. It had a telescopic aerial which could be moved about (as the salesman had explained) to get a perfect picture. When it was plugged in it came alive all right and set up a constant howl so unbearable that we had to keep the volume knob turned right down to make it possible to stay in the same room. The little screen gave a continuous display of ever-changing abstract shapes quite beyond the control of any of the battery of knobs and switches, and for no apparent reason it would burst suddenly into a firework display of such crackling intensity that we would run and pull the plug out before it blew up.

I trained (and actually qualified) as a radio mechanic in the army and went on a number of courses which involved the handling of lethal weaponry, but I had rarely been so nervous of any gadget as I was of that telly. We would spend perhaps half an hour in the corner of a room trying to bring it under control, then move it to some other spot, on top of the kitchen cupboard or under the bed, and try again. It was useless. I put it aside, as I had done with many another intractable object, until my brother, Alan, came down for a holiday. (He had learned to pack his overalls when he came to stay with us.)

Even he had trouble with it. In fact, half the trouble we had was his fault. If he had pronounced it beyond hope we could have put a foot through the front and used it as a toolbox. But he would not admit defeat. He produced a very long lead and carried the thing around the rooms while it was switched on. He would raise it above his head, swing it down to waist level and on near the floor, pirouetting over the wire to the left and chasséing to the right again when the lead became too twisted. He'd done a bit of ballroom dancing in his earlier years and it showed.

'I've got it, Norm,' he shouted suddenly. 'I think I've got it licked.' As he had passed it close to the window he had seen one and a half seconds of Sir Francis Chichester landing at Plymouth. The answer had struck him with the force of Newton's apple. 'It's the walls,' he said. 'the set is OK but the walls are hopeless. You see,' he explained, 'the walls are granite and are probably crammed with iron or tin or something. It'll never work on an indoor aerial but it should be great outside.'

We went out into the yard with three macs, one for him, one for me and one to keep the drizzle off the set. Plugged into the mains indoors, the lead went out through the window but it was not long enough to reach the ground outside. I held the set about two feet above the yard whilst he fiddled with the controls and went in and out to find screwdrivers and things. We could get a picture if I sat on the ground, leaned against the wall and balanced the set on top of my knees. The picture flew past at such a rate, however, that we

couldn't be sure what it was a picture of, but Alan was delighted. 'The signal's too weak down here,' he said. 'If we could get it up to the top floor of the mill and raise it above the walls it should be OK.' We went into town and got a set of batteries. They put weight on the set but freed us from the restriction of the mains lead.

There was no doubt that we got a better picture up there. It was so good that one was tempted to get interested in the programme but the set had to be held high above the head by someone, so it wasn't really satisfactory. The next step in Alan's scientific investigation was to take the thing on trial runs round the local countryside to see where it would work best. The next day we put it in the boot of the car and set off. We gathered a lot of interesting data. It would not work at all in ditches, we discovered, and the high stone walls on each side of the lanes gave us similar trouble to that encountered in the cottage. (Alan said that proved his metallic ore theory.) If we climbed onto the top of the walls we could get a recognizable picture after a bit of knob twiddling and some of the gateways proved good spots for viewing. Although it was fairly remote country a few people went by and, to our surprise, seemed fascinated. One chap, obviously a local, asked if we were from Rio Tinto and said we'd find nothing up there, '. . . and who the hell gave you permission to come prospecting round here anyway?' We explained that we were only testing our television set but he didn't seem convinced. At one point we were trapped in a gateway by a herd of shaggy cattle which a farmhand was driving along the lane. As they surged into the gateway Alan turned his back on them and held the squealing set over the gate for protection. 'Keep them off, Norm,' he kept shouting. 'Keep the devils off!' In another gap where the stone wall had collapsed, although we had to shade the screen from the sun to see it properly, we picked up a remarkably sharp picture of the weather man who told us that Cornwall was having thunderstorms.

We were, by then, in fairly high country but Alan felt we were still not getting enough elevation. He suggested that we might try wedging the set in the fork of a tree, which could be reached from the top of a wall. I put the set on the road whilst I gave him a leg-up and a car came round the corner and hit it. It flew off the road and disintegrated against the wall.

The driver squealed to a halt and got out looking a bit frightened. 'Are you all right?' he called. 'What did I hit?'

'It's OK. It was only the television set,' shouted Alan from the top of the wall. The man looked into his car and said something to his wife, then jumped back in and drove away, fast.

We never did have another television at the mill but it was a blessing in a way. It enabled Alan to give his full attention to finding out why we could only get French stations on the radio.

Mrs Marack was the wife of a farmworker who lived in a cottage a short distance along the lane from Penruin. We had an arrangement by which she checked on our cottage every two or three days to make sure that all was well. There was little other work for her to do apart from dusting and opening the windows from time to time to keep the place aired. Her husband, Dick Marack, trimmed the hedges and did a few other odd jobs about the place.

When Mr Pretty had completed the work inside the house, all the walls were covered with Kotina before decoration was applied. It is a thin film of expanded polystyrene which resists condensation by

keeping the surface of the walls warm. It was then covered with lining paper and all the rooms were colour washed. The effect was very pleasant; bright, clean and in keeping with the strong, simple feel of the building. The furniture, too, we kept as uncomplicated as possible, partly because it suited the cottage that way and partly because it cut down the amount of work necessary to keep it clean and in good order. Even when all was done, however, we found that when we went there to relax we worked harder than we did at home.

Most of this hard labour was concerned with cleaning and polishing the newly-laid slate floors and removing paint from the glass of the windows. We scratched, scraped and rubbed for hours at the thousands of drops of paint, varnish and colour wash which the workmen had scattered like coloured rain throughout the cottage. We spent a whole weekend on our knees in the main room alone, trying to remove the blobs of hardened cement which had been added to the splashes of colour. Every conceivable cleaner was tried but few were of any real use. Rhona read in a magazine that milk was ideal for the job so she put an extra bottle into the boot of the car when we went down next time. It was during one of our many crises with the water supply so we were also carrying a six-gallon plastic water container, which had a tap and a push-on lid about five inches in diameter.

On the way another car ran into our luggage boot when we stopped at traffic lights and sprang the lid of the compartment, so that we had to tie it down. When we arrived at Penruin we saw that there was little damage to the contents, but the spare bottle of milk had simply vanished without leaving any sign of broken glass or spilled contents. The lid was off the water container but not much had spilled. It was when we were making a cup of tea that we discovered the water was milky and that the extra bottle had jumped out of its own container and through the narrow neck into the water carrier. We had to economize with milk in our tea in order to keep enough to clean the floors. As a matter of fact it worked very well.

The windows, too, proved to be a nightmare of tedium and aching arms, for all the builder's promises had never produced a painter who could put the stuff on the woodwork alone. Sometimes the glass was worse to deal with than the Delabole slate because, after working away on a windowpane until our fingers went stiff, we frequently found that the offending spots were on the outside. Upstairs, after the rotten floorboards had been replaced, it was arranged that the floors should be treated with a sanding machine to bring them to a more or less even colour and that they should then be varnished. The snag was that after the sanding had been done the walls had been painted, which meant that the floorboards were liberally splashed with colour also. No effort had been made to remove the spots before the varnish was applied over the top, thus sealing them in likes flies in amber. After a few hours of trying to do something about these blemishes we gave up and admitted defeat. It was like trying to clean the colours out of a glass paperweight. We covered the floors with rush matting and went back to scraping windows.

Suddenly it was all over. The cottage was bright, neat and attractive from end to end. We had finished laying the staircarpet, hanging the curtains and pictures and choosing the ornaments we wanted. The hole in the bathroom ceiling was replastered and painted over so that it could hardly be seen. Even the new seat for the downstairs lavatory had been delivered at last and fixed proudly

in place. Our piece de resistance was a pair of white doves in delicate porcelain which we found in an antique shop in Truro and which now perched in quiet perfection on a little wooden corner shelf in the livingroom.

Mrs Marack was a quiet countrywoman, not given to sensationalism or emotional outbursts, so we were a bit concerned when we got her note. It read: 'Dear Mr and Mrs T, I have been to the mill and there is a mess. The black devils have got down the chimney and made mess and destruction. You will have to do something about the birds. Kind regards. Yours faithfully, Edith Marack. P.S. My husband has gone down.'

We went down too, in record time, and were stunned when we opened the door. The floors everywhere were covered once more with spots and the newly-painted walls were smeared all over by black wing-feathers, as if soot-grimed fingers had been drawn down them. There were concentrations of guano on the back of the settee, on the corner of the diningroom table and on the seats of the rail-back chairs. Broken crockery was scattered about the floors. Upstairs it was just as bad. The wardrobe door had obviously been a favoured perch, for dirty white rivulets had run down it both inside and out, as if the painters had been at work again. Several decorative china plates had been knocked from the walls and our white porcelain doves lay shattered on the dark slate floor.

It was a miserable sight but we were sadder still when we realized the plight of the wretched birds who had blundered into our cottage. There was no food or water there to sustain their weakening efforts to escape. The wallpaper and the Kotina beneath had been pecked away around every window, bearing mute testimony to their hopeless struggle to find freedom.

When we had cleaned up the cottage as well as we could, we swept the remains of our white doves into a dustpan and I took them outside to bury them. It was then, as I went through the orchard gate, that I caught sight of the tattered corpses of three jackdaws hanging by a piece of wire from the branch of an apple tree. Like all their kind, they must have been bright spirits as they floated in glossy black and grey on the vibrant air above the chimneystacks before their natural curiosity brought them to their frightful end.

It was infinitely sad to see them there, revolving slowly like broken criminals upon a gibbet. 'Why did you have to do it?' I asked them. 'Why did you have to explore the secret place you did not understand?'

'Because it was there,' they said, 'because it was there.'

I took them down and buried them with our white doves, where the buttercups were shining in the grass.

In spite of the delays and difficulties we had endured during the drawn-out saga of the cottage, Mr Pretty and his men rebuilt the mill wheel with both speed and skill. It was released from the silt and debris that gripped its lower edge and the trough was cleared of all obstructions. The interior cogs were already out of gear so that the wheel could turn freely on its axle without involving much of the gearing within. The sluice gate, which had once controlled the flow of water in the leat, had reached a state of advanced decay and was rebuilt. It could be operated from outside or inside the mill. What remained of the wooden paddles was removed from the slots in the cast iron rims and replaced by new elm boards, whilst the rotten spokes of the wheel, eight on either side, were renewed with seasoned oak. The axle and hub casings were cleaned and greased.

It was a symbolic moment when the family gathered in the yard to watch the great wheel turn again for the first time. Although the water which had escaped from the delapidated sluice had tumbled continuously through the fretted paddles, producing rainbows of sound and colour, the wheel itself had been a dead thing. It had protruded from the watery pit like the bones of some great dinosaur, exposed once more to the light of day by the inexorable processes of erosion. I felt like an important dignitary launching a ship or opening a new dam as I laid my hand upon the handle of the sluice. 'Pleasure and privilege . . .' I muttered, '. . . symbol of man's genius . . . Eternal struggle to harness the forces of nature. . . let us march forward . . . better world for our children. . .' and I swung the iron bar to port.

The water spouted in a smooth silver ark and broke into a thousand flying droplets on the paddles. The wheel seemed to tremble for a moment and then began to revolve slowly. The family leapt about cheering and I jumped down from the bank and joined them. We stepped backwards for some distance to view the broad scene like artists surveying their completed mural. It was a moving sight; as the wheel gathered momentum the dipping paddles threw up a sparkling corona of spray, an animated prism that split the sunlight into bands of vibrant colour.

It revolved there upon the dripping wall like a giant Catherine-wheel, flinging out showers of liquid fire to celebrate a moment of hope in its own long slide to dissolution. With no load to bear, no gears to mesh or heavy stones to turn, it was spinning far too fast but still I let it spin for long, long seconds before I lowered the gate and brought it back to quiet control and let it plod along, dipping its paddles to a slower rhythm. During the brief years that followed there were many hours of pleasure and contentment at Penruin; days of fishing in the bright waters of the river or painting in the lush meadows and on the wild moors, but I can remember nothing more deeply satisfying than the sight and sound of the wheel turning slowly in the foaming stream.

Some time later I foolishly repeated the ceremony when friends were staying. We gathered in the yard, I gave my speech, the bar was turned and the water spouted forth. The wheel moved forty-five degrees and stopped. I had no idea what had happened but my audience was reduced to helpless laughter. The water had suddenly disappeared down a large hole which had opened up in the bed of the leat, about ten feet behind the sluice gate. When I tried to explain what had happened they held on to each other squealing with delight. It was a disappointment, but those who were present on both occasions declared the second one to have been the most enjoyable.

The Bohemians

I cannot remember a time in my life when I did not have an all-consuming passion to draw and paint almost everything I saw. As an infant, long before I went to school, I can remember being irritated by the fact that whenever I asked for some paper to draw on adults would always produce a sheet or two of writing paper with lines on it. I do not think I ever saw a plain sheet of paper until I

went to school and I grew up thinking that adults saw the world through a horizontal grating. I was given paints in tins which always seemed to have the word 'Jumbo' or 'Giant' on the lid. Inside were multicoloured little rectangles of some hard substance which curled up at the corners after it had been attacked with the hairy-ended stick which was clearly designed to make the tin rattle rather than to persuade the little tablets to produce any colour. The only instructions I was given on the subject of fine art were to the effect that everything connected with it was deadly poisonous and that if I got it near my mouth I would die and that would be the end of that.

I mention these facts to show that, if my early introduction to the world of the visual arts was unable to put me off forever, then nothing I could experience later was likely to do so – and it never has. I have had other interests, of course, but none that has conflicted seriously with painting except for fishing which has caused me problems from time to time. The trouble is that when I go fishing I invariably find myself in surroundings that cry out to be painted and when I go to the same sort of area to paint, some wretched fish will ring the water surface and throw me into dithering indecision. I have tried often to combine the two pursuits but it is a mistake. I have abandoned a wash of colour on my sketching easel, grabbed my rod and chased upstream to cover a rising trout on more than one occasion but I have never caught the fish – or done a decent picture either. Once I had to abandon my rod and net and race back to scatter a herd of cows that was gathered around my painting gear and which had obviously decided that my efforts would be better trampled into the ground. The terrible truth was that their judgement was sound.

The result of all this has been that my closest personal friends are divided into two distinct groups and they rarely meet. Bob and Douglas fish but do not paint and I have spent many happy hours with both of them over the years. Ray and Harry paint but do not fish if they can help it, although I have known us often, on painting trips, to abandon sketch books for a game of boule, a skill which they rate higher by far than the piscatorial variety.

Both Ray and Harry are professional artists. Ray earns his living by selling original paintings and prints, whilst Harry is a designer producing posters and publicity of all kinds. He also paints. We three have met every Thursday at mid-day for many years at a quiet spot in the New Forest where we play a savage game of boule. Our excuse is that as we all work alone at home our lives can get a bit insular and, anyway, we need the exercise. The exercise is divided into two parts. During the first, we sit inside the camper van with a bottle of wine and some lunch and argue. Later we go outside into the sunshine, or rain, or snow and biting wind, and play this game of throwing heavy metal balls at a jack. The pitch we play on is ridiculous. It is a small tortuous little valley of sand, stones, fir cones and the droppings of the wild ponies that frequently stand about watching the game. We argue a lot in the second stage, also. John, who is a housemaster at a nearby college, joins us if his students have not set the dorm on fire or drowned in the college lake.

We also go on painting trips from time to time. This form of relaxation consists usually of me driving for a hundred miles or so in my van whilst my friends play pontoon or some other card game on the table behind me. They are not unfeeling and, from time to time, one or other will offer, with a pathetic whimper in his voice, to drive for a few miles if I am tired. They know I would never take the risk, so they are not taking much chance by offering. The only light relief I can get on this part of our outing is to wait for a long stretch of deserted road and slam the brakes hard on. I've been struck on the back of my head by flying pennies before now. But it's worth it.

When they heard that I had bought a watermill they were convulsed with laughter, even more so when I told them that I planned to restore it. They stopped laughing, however, when they realized that it could mean free holidays. On my assurance that paintings of my mill would sell like Mickey Mouse telephones, they became deadly serious and claimed priority over my fishing companions on the grounds that they would be staying at the mill for the sole purpose of earning a crust for their dependants, whilst Bob and Douglas had no other object but to frighten a few fish.

The truth is that all our dependants would have starved long ago if they had relied on our visits to the mill to provide sustenance, but we did paint when we could get round to it and if our pictures were hardly memorable, our visits were difficult to forget.

The routine of travel to Cornwall was much the same as to Wales or anywhere else where we journeyed to seek inspiration. They spent most of the time en route studying the latest hand they had been dealt, but it is only fair to add that they did not let all the landscape slip by without evaluating it with a professional artist's eye. From time to time one or other would cry 'Look! There's an eighty quidder' (or a hundred quidder, or whatever). I did not need to take

my eyes off the road ahead to know that they would be looking at the passing scene through their hands, forming a rough frame and estimating how much a painting of that particular view might sell for in a gallery. John was not an artist and, if he were with us, he would shout in protest, claiming that it was unsporting to break up a card game before he had won it and the other two would agree, with fake reluctance, to sacrifice their chance of riches rather than be considered cheats. By the time we had all agreed not to stop, the piece of landscape in question was miles behind us anyway.

We did, however, stop quite often upon Dartmoor to make drawings of the rocks, cottages and bridges or climb upon the tors to look at the long views and watch the cloud shadows compose and recompose the landscape in ever-changing patterns of tone and colour. It was on the bank of the East Dart river that I painted the only picture I have ever made which refused to dry. I have never understood the reason for that particular phenomenon. It was not a damp day, the sun was shining and the paper was dry. I used no more water than usual but an hour after I had put on the first touch of colour, that touch was still as wet as ever. I tried to keep the areas of paint apart by leaving a thin line of untouched paper between them but I was quite unable to control the materials in any way. Finally they had all fused together so completely that it was quite impossible to tell what the soggy mess was intended to represent. I abandoned it at last among the icecream papers and plastic bags in a litter bin near Postbridge. Harry and Ray still claim that it was the best piece of work I ever did.

We stopped sometimes for a quick game of boule when we came upon a suitable pitch but we were always inclined to stay too long on these occasions and our already very elastic timetable would become chaotic. Once, when we were still on our way at two o'clock in the morning, we were stopped by a police car in a dark country lane. The constables wanted to know who we were and where we came from and where we were going and why. After going over us all with torches they finally let us go. But they made no pretence of believing our story that we were innocent artists looking for inspiration, who had become benighted by misjudging the time we had spent playing boule on Dartmoor.

There was plenty of subject matter to paint at the mill and along the river valley but, north of Penruin, where the sloping valley side gave way to moorland, the landscape changed abruptly and the atmosphere of the countryside changed with it. Here was a starker, more elemental world with new excitements for landscape painters, for within a few miles one emerged into a rugged, mysterious and strangely frightening country. The light on the lonely moors flowed along like a silent river and the mood of the bald hills and craggy tors would slip in moments from clear and open to close and threatening. The mists seemed to rise like phantoms from the earth itself and disappear as suddenly as if sucked back through the dark crevices of the looming cairns. Great rock formations, sunlit against the long, breathtaking distances would be transformed by a mere cloud shadow to glowering menace and monoliths of ancient granite became wizards and warlocks. The fissures of the tumbled crags changed in the shadows to runic signs and esoteric symbols of half-forgotten pagan rites.

The orchard at Penruin was full of enchantment and gentle charm, but up there in the high and lonely places charms and enchantment had a very different meaning. For that was a land of ancient superstition and wild imaginings. The earth-mother still moved her great body there beneath the tussocky grass and the wind sighed like a hollow organ-peal between the rocks. Men had lived there in the Stone Age and left mysterious circles of standing stones for me to rest my sketching tools on and to touch me as I worked, almost hand to hand across four thousand years and more. It was not difficult then to believe that the spirits of the long-dead tinners, who streamed those rocks for precious ores since the age of bronze, still haunted the bleak landscape. The later tin miners knew these spirits, so they said, and saw and heard them still, as they went about their own gruelling work. They took the form of evil goblins, ugly and malicious, and the miners claimed that they sometimes found their small, primitive tools in remote rocky clefts and heard them knocking in the Stygian darkness of the mine shafts and subterranean passages. To disturb these creatures was to bring ill luck and, if one was unfortunate enough to meet one face to face, the knacker (which is what the miners called them) would change instantly to an ugly black goat and disappear among the rocks.

Strange beliefs and superstitions have endured in Cornwall through the centuries, abetted by the hard reality of symbolic stones and temples. Stories may still be heard in those parts of curses which have more power than prayer, of charms and spells and spirits in the sacred wells. I watched hard and long for a hare to

run upon the moor to see if it were white with burning eyes, for then I would have known it to be the spirit of some long-dead tinner or, more likely, of a witch. But I never saw one, nor came across a nest of adders basking on the warm rocks.

It was not wise to wander far from the roads for, whether one was superstitious or not, the oozing bogs were real enough and I had no desire to find out whether they really were bottomless. It was an odd thought that the water in these marshy depressions, sinister and dangerous as it was, might be the same which later would spout, clear and limpid, in my orchard spring at Penruin and, if I had primed the pump correctly, might run into the basin when I washed my face.

But the moors had other ghosts than these, more recent but hardly less remote from my own life. They were there, unbelievably, in their hundreds and even thousands, tramping the hidden pathways through the scrubland to the now deserted mines. All that I could see was the engine houses, their ruined arches and gaunt chimneys in the grip of clinging ivy. Sometimes it seemed to me as easy to believe that goblins and black goats still haunted the rocks as that hundreds had once worked below these lonely ruins, making it in early days the most concentratedly industrial area of Britain.

The engine houses were remote and beautiful, romantic as mediaeval castles and as fascinating as ancient tombs, but their attraction was enhanced by the cosmetic action of time and the strangely comforting power of nature to overcome all man-made things and gather them once more within itself. For they were but the symbols of the unbelievable drudgery which man will endure to win what he conceives to be the desirable treasures of the earth. I found it difficult to believe, in those lonely and forbidding places, that so many generations of streamers and miners had toiled for centuries in those very spots and that they had gone like a passing dream because richer deposits of copper and tin had come to light as far away as Africa and Malaya. It is possible that mining may begin again at some future time, but I feel sure that the symbolic stones which I leaned upon to work will still be there when the engine houses and my ephemeral drawings have long crumbled into dust.

Sometimes when we were staying at the mill to paint we would work along the rocky coastline or in the uniquely beautiful fishing ports and harbours and, sometimes, upon the moors. One day when we were up there, the moorland was brooding in a thin mist which covered tedious detail and divided the hills and rocks into simple, powerful washes of subtle colour. We were driving slowly, looking for some point of interest which would offset the stark simplicity of the landscape, when Harry yelled and pointed to a little recess in the bald slope of the hillside. 'Look,' he said, 'there's gravel there, flat gravel. Let's have a couple of games of boule. We might not find another decent bit of ground all day.' It didn't seem a bad idea at the time. It was early still and we had plenty of time to paint.

The ground was certainly very good: flat gravel, as Harry had said, inside a small quarry-like recess in the shoulder of the moor. We were a bit disappointed to find the centre of the arena occupied by a sheep which had been dead a long time, but the chances of finding another pitch as good without a dead sheep seemed remote. I don't recall how many games we played there that day but we had our lunch and continued into the afternoon. Finally, the mist began to close in until we could see less detail of the landscape than we would have liked. Any paintings we might have done after that would have been reduced to little more than a single grey wash, so we reluctantly gave up the idea. It would be a mistake to imagine that we did not care about getting no work done. On the contrary, we all made quite detailed drawings of the dead sheep before we returned to Penruin, although it is doubtful whether we would have had the nerve to study our silent spectator so closely if he had turned out to be an ugly black goat.

We stopped once to play near a river but a sudden burst of brilliant shooting by Ray carried both the jack and his own ball about ten yards out into deep water and the game had to be called off. It was a picturesque spot, however, so we all settled down to painting within a hundred yards or so of each other. A month or two later we realized that we had each sold the pictures we painted that day.

One of the essential ingredients of our sketching tours has always been that we should enjoy good food. We take some trouble to avoid the sort of establishment where the proprietors think of it merely as fuel. We were making a short trip from the mill to the coast one day when we discovered a marvellous pub. The beer was excellent and the food no less desirable. There was a wide choice on the menu and we all ordered what we wanted and settled down to a leisurely meal. Ray has fairly catholic tastes but he also has a strange craving for rice, only the best rice of course, but there is a tendency for his plate to look like a piece of landscape in the china clay area. I did not hear what he ordered from the menu that day and I was idly watching his white pyramid to see what would come to light when a large spider heaved itself out of the top like a workman emerging from a manhole cover. It sat there shining for a moment or two like a black cherry on a meringue before my strangled scream got out.

The management did all they could, short of throwing screens around our table and prostrating themselves beneath our feet. The head waiter was offering Ray anything he cared to ask for, free of charge, and the lady of the house was gripping his hand and looking as if she was going to kiss him all the way up his arm. The excitement must have upset the spider which was making desperate attempts to get back under the rice. We all felt genuinely sorry for the staff and Ray, in his good-natured way, assured them that it was not the end of the world and that a different choice from their excellent menu would be sufficient recompense. They almost carried him away behind the scenes to choose food to his heart's content. He emerged a few minutes later with his face covered in smiles and his newly selected dish covered by yet another mountain of rice. When we got back to the mill that night I went through the store cupboard, took out a packet of rice and hammered it with the poker before throwing it out for the birds.

Harry always maintains, quite rightly, that one should never fail to compliment any member of the catering trade who gives good food and service and he is always at pains to practice what he preaches. He is equally fervent about letting both management and staff know when they fall seriously short of reasonable standards. This attitude is, no doubt, what is known as 'a good thing' but it can produce unexpected results. One complication is that when we are on painting trips our clothing is sometimes a little unorthodox and few people seem to connect us with the Egon Ronay set. A surly waitress once referred us to a lorry drivers' pull-in down the road before we had decided whether the hotel we had entered came up to our requirements. It could have been the frayed peak of my deerstalker, or Harry's moth-eaten flying jacket from the last war (he was in the army as a matter of fact), or John's pullover with Royal Naval Lifeboat Institute in red letters on the front, that misled the young lady, but it was no way to treat artistic gourmets.

It was Harry's determination to reform slack caterers that led to his acquiring the nickname of 'Bacon-boots'. We had stopped at a fairly impressive hotel for a quick drink but before continuing on our way to do some work along the rocky coastline, we decided to pass a few minutes on the putting green outside. It was a fascinating little course. Ray is quite handy with a golf club whilst I frequently get from the tee to the green without ever touching the fairway. Harry refuses to play the game at all on the grounds that everyone who holds a golfclub is a snob, including us. This course, however, was so uneven that it brought everybody's abilities down to the same level. In fact the tussocks of coarse grass around the holes made putters obsolete and one had to try chipping straight into the holes even from a foot away. It was great fun and we stayed too long.

The upshot was that we decided to stay the night and make an early start the next day. Dinner that evening was among the worst we have ever eaten. Every item was straight from the freezer and retained the shape of the packet it had come from. 'Oh God, even the waitresses are square,' wailed Harry. He called for the head waiter and told him what he thought. He was polite enough and his description of the meal was accurate to a degree but the waiter was not amused. The next morning we sat down to breakfast and I detected a new air of respect from the waitress who had, no doubt, been warned to handle the troublemakers with tact. All went well until Harry noticed that we had two rashers of bacon and he only had one.

'You must have eaten it,' we suggested.

'I have *not* eaten it,' said Harry, beginning to suspect some sort of plot. He called the waitress and pointed out the discrepancy.

'You must have eaten it, sir,' she said. 'Every full English breakfast has two rashers, sir.'

'I have *not* eaten it,' said Harry, starting to twitch. The young lady did not risk further argument; she took away his plate and returned a minute later with two rashers and all the trimmings.

'The chef sends his apologies, sir,' she said. 'He cannot account for such an oversight.'

Harry was climbing back into the car outside when Ray pointed to something flapping from the sole of his shoe. It was a full English rasher of bacon.

Harry had another strange habit about that time. He took to carrying a pocket chess set about with him wherever he went. When he could get an odd moment he would take it out and pore over it, grunting and chuckling to himself and pushing the little chess men into this hole and that, like a witch pushing pins into a wax doll. I caught him at it several times in dark corners of the mill when it was his turn to brush the mud off the staircarpet in the cottage; once or twice when he was sitting at his easel in the fields making out that he was painting; and once in a clump of bushes just off the A30 where we supposed he had gone for a more urgent reason. He dropped his chess set in the water when he was having a bath at Penruin and it took him nearly an hour to dry it out properly on the kitchen stove.

The motive behind this strange ritual was to invent awkward situations for unsuspecting chess players to get themselves into and, when he conjured up a really nasty one, he would send it off to the then *Manchester Guardian* so that they could drive their readers mad trying to get out of it. We were surprised and impressed to find that a number of these problems were published and we wondered whether any of the sufferers ever dreamed that their tortures were sometimes dreamed up during protracted sessions in the downstairs loo of a Cornish watermill.

Harry's habit of indulging in this odd pastime at any moment of the day meant that he frequently forgot where he had left his chess set when his attention had been diverted to other things. On one occasion we had to turn the car round and go back several miles to recover it from the harbour wall at Mevagissey and, on another, we rescued it (in a lightning raid) from under a table of a cafe in Tintagel, where Harry had had an altercation with the proprietor earlier that day about her slipshod handling of the soup. The matter came to a head after we had heard him muttering to himself in bed at about two o'clock in the morning. He continued to study his board throughout breakfast and helped us to pack the car for the day's painting, with bits of luggage in one hand and his chess board in the other. We were just backing out of the yard when Harry yelled for Ray to stop. 'I've left it on the car roof,' he cried. We all piled out of the car but the chess set had gone. We found the little box which contained the board near where the car had been parked, but a wheel had gone over it and most of the chess men were missing. We found some of them flattened on the path but most of them had to be prised out of the tyre treads with a screwdriver. Harry was a bit morose for a day or two but the incident seemed to have broken him completely of the habit. I have not heard him mention chess (or the *Manchester Guardian*) from that day to this.

Ray did all the cooking when we ate our meals at the mill, and very skilful he was at it, too. On one of our trips he came in his own van and brought his two teenage children with him. He did not flinch at the idea of cooking for six of us and refused all offers of help. He supplemented the burners on the scullery cooker by lighting the pressure stove in his vehicle in the mill yard, and was not in the least put out by the fact that they were almost thirty yards apart. I have never seen a smoother operation than that first meal he cooked. He moved from the saucepans bubbling in the scullery, through the room where we all sat around the table, into the hallway and through the door and out across the yard to stir another pan that hissed outside. He would give it his expert attention for a few moments and set off back the way he came to catch something on the other cooker just in time, then back again with seasoning or herbs or pinch of salt, then back again to put the plates to warm or stir the gravy.

The rest of us watched in amazement, our heads moving in unison this way and that as if we were at the centre court at Wimbledon. Every time Ray passed through the scullery door he hit his head with a resounding bang on the low lintel. We shouted warnings but he didn't seem to hear them, he was so engrossed. He went on pacing back and forth and cracked his head each time and so we all swore in unison at every impact. It was the least we could do to help a friend.

We met a lot of interesting characters on our travels both in Cornwall and other places too, and somehow they have all become interwoven with the drawings, notes and sketches that we made along the way. It may be that one's awareness of the world is heightened during the process of recording visual things with pencil, pen or brush. For most people the family photograph album or a batch of holiday snaps can be a great delight. They are to me, but sketchbooks and paintings, even the slightest notes, can recall not just the day and place but the hour, the moment, the sounds and smells that would have gone forever without them. I have drawings still which I did as a child and I can remember when I come across them what my brother said to me, what my mother was doing at the time, what was on the radio when I was working and how I felt about the world that day.

From time to time I come across a little pencil sketch of two bridges, one above the other, which I did on one of our jaunts in central Wales some years ago, and I can feel the wind on my face and smell the trees and hear old David's voice. I can hear the tyres slipping on the stony path up to the beautiful, rambling old house on the hillside where we were staying. It was owned by a frail and elderly couple, a delightful pair, kindly and amusing and so eccentric that our short stay became an experience to remember. The rooms of the house, which were so numerous that we often lost our way, varied wildly in their size and contents. Some were divided by rough partitions into smaller sections which seemed to have no purpose. There was a sink in one and nothing else except a perfect chest of ancient oak with linen-fold carving as genuine as I have ever seen. There were two great grandfather clocks on the staircase and another at the foot, crowded against a Jacobean table, long and massive, where heavy candelabra, silver jugs and teapots were piled in heaps, loosely wrapped in torn and yellowing newspapers. Some rooms were bare and dismal and others crowded with old furniture and bric-à-brac like an antique dealer's dream.

We chatted with the old couple the first evening in their gloomy livingroom where they served us sherry from a magnificent tantalus of heavy cut-glass decanters with silver chains and nameplates and then romped like children with their little dog, hugging and kissing him and squeaking with delight. A dim tapestry hung loosely on one wall depicting richly dressed gentlemen on horseback, one with a

Trethevy Quoit

hooded hawk upon his gauntlet, all galloping with long thin greyhounds at their heels through stately trees. 'Do you like it?' asked the old lady, seeing my interest. I said I did, indeed. 'Show the boys your new one, David,' she said to her husband and he went away without a word. Some minutes later he returned, staggering backwards through the door, hauling an enormous roll of dark material along the floor. We rushed to his assistance and were astonished at the size and weight of the limp and dusty object as we tried to turn it through the door. Once in the room the two old people began to unroll their prize exhibit. It was far too big for the crowded floor space but they went on unrolling over chairs and tables whilst clouds of dust billowed from the musty roll. We could see little enough of the original design on the faded surface which swamped the room and most of its contents beneath turgid waves of woven fabric. We murmured our admiration of vague details here and there, and made a mental note to show no interest in the piles of rolled up carpets which loomed in dark uncharted corners of the house. We slept in one great barn-like room. I was horrified to find another tapestry behind my bed, carelessly attached to the plaster by rusty tacks so that it sagged above my pillow like washing on a clothes-line. I got into bed with care and prayed that the tacks would hold until the morning.

One wing of the room was partitioned off to form two other small compartments. One was a kitchen with a sink and cupboards and a window which allowed a dim green light to filter through the encroaching leaves. The other, inner compartment, contained a bath and water geyser which looked like some vague relic of the distant war which might be encountered sticking from the sand of a beach in Normandy. We breakfasted on a Regency drum table in the bay window. The table top rocked back and forth upon its pedestal as we shared our box of cornflakes and gazed through the window at the breathtaking view. After breakfast Ray decided to have a bath and I to wash the dishes in the kitchen, whilst Harry disappeared to make a few drawings from the antiques. I could hear Ray's appalling singing voice through the cardboard wall as I sluiced the dishes and I heard him pull the bath-plug. The hair stood out on the back of my neck as my feet were immersed in a sudden rush of hot soapy water. 'My God, Ray!' I shouted. 'What are you doing? The bath water's coming through the wall.' There was a scuffle behind the partition and he appeared at the kitchen door, stark naked and dripping with water. 'What the hell . . .?' he said, his eyes popping at the water still flooding in like the foaming edges of spent waves on the beach. I was jumping about, trying to get past him but it was too late – my shoes were squelching with the warm water which had overwhelmed them.

Ray grabbed a towel, tied it round his waist and went running off into the hall, still scattering water in his wake. I heard his bare feet pounding up the staircase. It seemed a long time before he came back. I had wrung out my socks and put them with my shoes to dry outside and the bathwater had, unbelievably, drained away through the outer wall by then as if it were sponge. The oilcloth was still wet and steaming when Ray returned, and so was he.

'Bloody funny place, this,' he said. 'I found them in a bedroom and when they called me in they were still in bed, tiny and frail as little kids, and the dog was lying in between them with his nose over the counterpane.'

'What did they *say*, Ray? What about the bathwater?' I insisted.

'Oh that. They just said don't worry about it. It's always doing that.'

One morning at Penruin, when Ray and Harry were in the field above the orchard trying to persaude a herd of nervous sheep to pose for them, I wandered off along the bank until I came to the point where the mill stream returned its borrowed water to the river. The sluice gate was closed and the wheel idle against the wall, so that the stream was clear and almost unruffled as it slid along. When the gate was open it rushed along, slapping and leaping between the mossy boulders, baffling the eye, but in repose it exposed its secrets with limpid clarity. I had often waded along it from the river's edge, between its grassy banks to where the snagging arms of brambles and wild roses concealed the culvert opening below the yard. I did so again that morning, stopping every pace or two to watch for living things. It was early autumn and the soft pale disc of the sun was trying to burn through the curtain of translucent haze. The air was golden and the trees were faded olive-green with patches of ochre yellow and warm sienna. Crinkled leaves, their edges curled like gay boats of Christmas paper, floated slowly down the stream, twisting and turning between the boulders until they reached the river where the stronger current snatched them away to join a hundred others on their journey to the sea. A scattering of rooks was drilling the pasture, framed beneath the curving bellies of dairy cows grazing beyond the tangled hedge. I could hear their tongues tearing the grass and smell their warm scent on the still moist air.

Wading alone along the stream, watching the pebbles for fish and plant and insect life, held for me all the magic of the childhood rockpools by the sea where we waded with our threepenny nets, watching near our own pink toes for scuttling crabs and shrimps, and wondering at the strange distortion of our infant legs. The little creatures in the tailrace were difficult to see, lying barred and speckled among the stones. I crouched down every pace or two watching for swimming beetles, sliding snails and limpets, or the sudden movement of the tiny trout, or loaches flat as a miller's thumb. So rapt I was that I hardly noticed the increased movement of the stream until a small tidal wave of clear cold water caught me unawares, swamping my wellingtons and wetting my trousers up beyond my knees.

I heard the strangled laughter as I leaped out and scrambled up the bank and saw them peering round the corner of the mill. I found them sitting on the low stone wall beside the open sluice gate and set them rocking with fresh laughter as I poured the water from my boots. 'Don't worry about it,' they kept shrieking, patting me across the shoulder, 'Don't worry about it. It's always doing that.'

Sometimes we travelled in Ray's van which had a sliding door and rattled like a tin full of spanners. Although I enjoy the convenience of travelling by road, I do not like driving, but Ray is both confident and expert at the wheel whether he is wending his way through the terrifying traffic of central London or rolling like a rally driving ace through the narrow lanes or precipitous hillsides of the West Country. On one trip we took a single bed down to the mill with us to supplement the sleeping capacity. The vehicle was already crammed with easles, boxes of painting gear, three or four sets of boule balls, tins of food, loaves of bread and milk bottles, a four-gallon water container and Ray's dog. The mattress was doubled over and also crammed inside. It kept trying to open itself out, so that the metal frame of the bed spring, with its criss-cross wire mesh, was pushed up against the roof of the van where it beat an ear-splitting tattoo as soon as the engine was switched on. There was only room for one passenger by the driver so, as the smallest member of our expedition, it was decided (by the other two) that I should go in the back with the spaniel.

I will never forget that nightmare journey. I don't think my hearing has ever been the same since. On the whole, Ray is a good-natured sort of chap but my cries of agony, muffled as they were by my attempts to get my head under the mattress, seemed to spur him on to renewed efforts to squeeze a yard more speed out of the old banger. I was grateful to his dog that day; he didn't panic even when the boule balls broke loose, but he was no fool either and got a lot further into the folded mattress than I did and filled my mouth with dog-hairs on the way. The wire mesh above my head swayed and banged until I was sure that any moment I was going to be diced like a tinned carrot.

There was just one bright spot on that journey. As we were careering round the tight corners of the narrow lanes I realized that Harry's laughter had died away and I peered over the shifting cargo. He was pressed backwards in his seat with his feet braced tight against the dashboard, his head was thrust back and he was holding his hat over his eyes. 'Bend your knees, Harry,' I yelled. 'You'll go straight through the front if he slams the brakes on.'

'Give me a go in the back, Norm,' he shouted. 'Fair's fair!'

'Not likely,' I bawled. 'It's great back here inside the mattress.' But I don't think he heard the snoring noises above the din.

By chance I was with Harry and Ray the last time I saw Penruin.

They gave me the sketches they made that morning and I have them still, along with my own. When I look at them, brief as they are, I can remember that Sunday morning in a far-off summer as if it were yesterday. It was nearly time to go and we were leaning back against the gnarled trunks in the orchard. The sun was hot and grasshoppers were chirping all around us in the lush grass. I can smell the pungent docks and nettles against the bleached side of the old chicken house and see the wild briar roses by the gate. A foam of creamy-white elder flowers leaned from the hedge below the spring. Swallows skimmed the pale blue sky and scythed through the nebula of gnats that danced between the apple trees. We had to go at last, of course, but nothing lasts for ever and at least I have those sketches still.

Angler's Glory

I have nothing to show for the many pleasant days I spent fishing on the river except a few small black and white snaps and a fund of recollections which I would not swap for a twenty-pound salmon on the end of a fly line. I had been fishing on various lakes and rivers for many years before we discovered the mill and Bob and Douglas had been my constant companions on these trips. It cannot be claimed that we were ever a wildly successful trio and we certainly caught nothing at Penruin that we could boast about, but we added many glorious days to our collection of fishing memories and were content. Most of our fishing talk still takes place in the pub on Friday evenings as it has done for many years now. It is a surprising fact that all the best memories are of the unsuccessful days when nothing seemed to go right. Like the day on the Dorset Stour when

Bob arrived without wellingtons or waders and was forced to reach fishable water beyond the riverside reeds by walking out along a fallen tree trunk. It was solid and heavy and looked as if it had lain in the water's edge for years. He was very pleased with his good fortune, having thought that his lack of boots would spoil his day's sport and he was already making his first casts to rising dace when the log began to roll.

He managed to keep his balance by taking a pace forward as the log turned but, unfortunately, his efforts to stay on board became more desperate and the log began to speed up. He performed a remarkable display of acrobatics and was running like a hamster in an exercise wheel when his shoe slipped on the wet wood. I have never quite understood why one laughs in such a situation. I could not understand why Douglas and I were still laughing when we dragged Bob backwards through the reeds with mud up to our own knees. Since that day it has needed only the mention of tree trunks to set us all off again, squeaking with laughter, including Bob. The mere catching of a fish could never match such an occasion for enjoyment.

One of the many endearing characteristics which make Douglas such a good companion is his ability to remain unruffled in situations which would throw most of us into a frenzy of frustration. This enviable trait was obviously granted to him by nature to compensate for the fact that he is prone to minor accidents. In fact, if there is an accident about, you can bet your life that Douglas will have it, and he will remain calm both whilst he is having it and while things are being cleared up afterwards. I have known him to remain tranquil with a hook embedded so deeply in the point of his chin that the barbed point had emerged at the other end. He didn't get upset when we tried, and failed, to get it out for him, or when we had to pack up fishing and get him to a doctor. I'm ashamed to admit that Bob and I did begin to lose our cool a bit when the doctor couldn't manage the job either and sent us all off to the cottage hospital where the operation was successfully carried out. Douglas saw us both safely home after the incident. I don't think he would have mentioned being hooked whilst we were still fishing had it not been for the fact that the chap who hooked him was about twenty yards downstream, facing in the opposite direction and, thinking that he was caught up in a tree branch, continued to pull on his fly line until he had almost yanked Doug out of his wellingtons.

He did not carry any more gear than we did when we were fishing and he was most careful about attaching each item securely to his person, but nothing would ever stay secured for long. We gradually took to walking behind him so that we could pick up each object as it fell away. This was not so much a self-sacrificing attitude on our part as an attempt to cut down the time spent going back to search for items which he lost when we were off our guard.

One late summer evening when the sun had gone down and we were putting our tackle into the car to go home, Douglas announced that he had lost one of his waders. If he had lost both there would have been nothing unusual about it, but Bob and I could never understand how he could lose one big, heavy wading boot when one of his legs was still in the other. He swears to this day that he has no idea what became of it. My fishing companions are less volatile than the Bohemians but even they can act strangely at times. Once, when we were all three fishing quite near to each other on the Test, a herd of inquisitive young cattle gathered round me and forced me nearer and nearer to the edge of the bank. They could both see well enough what was happening and hear my shouts but they simply stood there watching with broad grins on their faces until I slid into the water, and then hooted with laughter as they scattered the cattle and helped me out. They claim it was one of the high points in their fishing experiences.

Douglas still has this strange inability to keep in touch with his fishing tackle but remains to this day a delightful, easy-going companion and one of those comparatively rare men who one would instinctively turn to in times of real trouble or distress. I fished with him once for a whole week in Wales. We were after salmon and we threshed the water from early morning until late evening every day without a single bite between us, and yet I cannot recall a moment of boredom.

Both Douglas and Bob were agog to hear that I had acquired the mill and when I told them about the wild brown trout in the river, the shoals of sea-trout in the millpool and the good runs of salmon in the estate agent's blurb, they could hardly wait to get there, whether the cottage was habitable or not. I could not bear to think of what might happen if we all got down there while there were still holes in the bedroom floors which we might get our legs down, or hooks in the pig room ceiling which could get caught in the lobes of our ears, so I made various excuses to keep them at a safe distance until the place was more or less accident-proof. The time arrived, however, when I could keep them away no longer.

It took us over seven hours to drive down and we arrived about mid-afternoon. They piled out of the car as soon as it stopped in the yard and hardly glanced at the mill.

'Where's this mill pool?' they called, dragging their tackle out of the car boot. 'Did you say you could see the sea-trout?'

'Yes,' I replied. 'Hang on a minute, let's have a cup of tea first.' But they were off down the mill leat, hung with tackle like animated Christmas trees. 'It's about a quarter of a mile away,' I yelled, but they took no notice as they struggled through the barbed-wire fence which divided my fields from those of my neighbour.

When I think of the number of years that I have been fishing I am astonished at my own naivety in believing that if fish can be seen they can also be caught. The truth is that I don't really believe it but, much as I longed for a cup of tea and a rest after the long drive, I knew I would be unable to relax for one second whilst there remained even the remotest chance that my friends might clear the sea-trout from my pool while I was skulking indoors. I therefore grabbed my own tackle from the car and hurried after them. I got tangled up on the barbed wire in my haste and picked up Douglas's net a few yards further on, but I managed to get to the pool only minutes behind them. Bob was shading his eyes and looking down into the deep, clear water. 'My God!' he kept muttering. 'Just look at the beauties.' Douglas was sitting on the bank a few yards away calmly fitting his rod together. There was not a strand of weed in the water to obscure our view of the trout. They were lying in three groups on the sandy shoals between the rocks at the bottom, about sixteen fish in all, as motionless as three flotillas of submarines lurking on the ocean floor.

The pool was difficult to fish because it was more or less surrounded by trees and the few gaps between them were a bit restricted for casting a fly. The best place, therefore, from which to fish was along the edge of the dam itself, for it was reasonably easy to make a long back-cast there without getting caught up in the tree branches. Douglas was the first to get himself tackled up and ready to start. His rod was both new and newly repaired, a circumstance which only he could bring about. Hearing that the then newly-invented fibreglass rods were as strong as steel and virtually indestructible, he had discarded his old, much-repaired cane rod and invested in a shining new glass one a month or two earlier. Unfortunately, as we were starting out on a fishing trip designed mainly (as far as Doug was concerned) to test his new rod, he had inadvertently slammed the car door before his rod was fully inside

April 1972
Horse Chestnut

and had chopped it off about four inches above the cork handle. His old cane rod was not available either because, having been lulled into a false sense of security by possessing a new one, he had used it to ease a loose slate off the edge of an outhouse. It came off easily enough but in his effort to get out of the way when it fell, he had splintered the end of the rod on the rough brick wall. The upshot of these little accidents was that he had only a short spinning rod still in service and he was forced to spin with a huge metal spinner to ensure, as far as possible, that he would not catch a trout by unfair means. The maddening thing was that Bob and I didn't see a trout all day and Douglas hauled in a very nice pike.

The manufacturers of Douglas's new rod wrote that they had never heard before of a glass rod coming apart in anyone's hand, but they were jealous of their reputation and had returned the rod to him 'as new' a few weeks before our trip to the mill. The slippery edge of the dam was not a particularly safe place to stand, especially with two or three inches of water sliding over it, but with Douglas in the centre sending a needle-sharp hook whistling back and forth at about three hundred miles per hour, it was hazardous in the extreme, so that Bob and I chose the gaps between the trees from which to fish. We could not quite see him from where we stood.

Those sea trout showed not the slightest interest in us or our flies and we were both struggling to extract our hooks from surrounding trees when we noticed Douglas sitting calmly on the bank behind us. 'What are you doing there?' we asked.

'Waiting for you two,' he replied. 'I could murder a cup of tea.' He lifted his rod, a piece in each hand. 'Fell apart after a couple of casts,' he said, with the air of one who knows his fate and has resigned himself to it.

We stayed long enough to lose a few more trout-flies in the overhanging branches and to shout abuse at the fish that tantalized us before making our way back to the mill. 'I don't know what I'm

going to tell the manufacturers,' Douglas groaned. 'I can hardly say it came apart in my hand again, but this time it really did.'

'Why not tell them you accidentally slammed the car door on it?' suggested Bob. We had reached the cottage door when I realized I was still carrying Douglas's landing net.

Bob was volunteer cook on our fishing expeditions and, although he was not in Ray's class as a chef, he did very well in spite of his predilection for serving up frozen fish fingers. He produced a few disastrous breakfasts from time to time but this was due almost entirely to his habit of communing with nature at all sorts of odd moments. He would put the bacon and sausages into the pan on the cooker and walk out of the door to stare dreamily at the idyllic landscape or check what the birds were doing on such a fine morning. He rarely came to his senses until he noticed blue smoke issuing from the open doorway. His utensils never actually caught fire, as far as I remember, but I do recollect our entire bacon ration being turned to a fine brown dust one morning.

It must be said, however, that he was always first up in the mornings and, being a thoughtful companion, usually brought a cup of tea for Douglas and me. It was tea to remember, so strong and sweet that it almost glued our tongues to the roofs of our mouths. We daren't go to sleep again for fear of choking.

In the evenings we often walked along the lane to the pub by the river, and a very cosy place it was. We were a bit surprised to find that the locals knew who we were at our first visit and knew also that we were there for the fishing. (They were a little puzzled when I went there with the Bohemians, I thought, but that was not surprising.) They knew the river well too and didn't hesitate to advise us on where the best fish were likely to be found. They congratulated me on owning the best sea-trout pool for miles around and wished us the best of luck with it, but they did not hesitate to reminisce also with much loud laughter about the golden days when they had taken fish from under the very nose of old Tom Brydon. Tom, it seemed, had owned the pool for many years, but had never really understood the best technique for fishing it and they had not enlightened him. They skilfully avoided giving us any clues also, but the fact that they never asked us directly whether we had caught any of the sea-trout indicated clearly enough that they already knew.

The real trouble with the mill pool was that it was a difficult and rather dangerous place to fish even in daylight, and we were reluctant to risk our necks on those slippery rocks at night, which is the right time to fish for sea-trout. The technique which had baffled old Tom was certainly not the kind which one would be likely to learn from books, but I must admit that I would dearly have liked to know what it was.

One evening, when we were walking back home from the river pub, Douglas hinted that he might try a bit of night fishing. The air was warm and balmy and the moon round and full. Wild flowers were lush in the high rank grass on each side of the lane and glow-worms were like scattered sparks in the wild fuchsia. Between the black trunks of the trees silver sheep grazed quietly on silver fields.

'No reason why you shouldn't, Douglas,' I said. 'There are three spare rods in the mill.'

'Don't encourage him,' said Bob. 'The mind boggles at what might happen if he goes down there alone. It's risky enough in broad daylight.'

'Well! I wouldn't want to think of you worrying about me,' said Douglas. 'Who's got the bottle of whisky?' Half an hour later we were drifting off to sleep.

I was awakened the next morning by Bob with a cup of tea. 'Doug has disappeared,' he announced anxiously. 'I've been up since six and there's no sign of him.' The idea of Douglas night fishing alone on the edge of the dam brought me to full wakefulness in seconds and I dressed hurriedly. Douglas's fishing bag and one of the spare rods had gone. We were about to chase off down to the mill pool when Bob said 'Don't panic! There he is.' He was pointing through the window.

It was a relief to see Doug in spite of the fact that he was in the gateway of the river field trying to extract the delicate tip of the trout rod from a hawthorn bush. Bob threw open the window and shouted,

'Leave it where it is, man. We'll cut the bush down.' But Douglas affected not to hear.

When we emerged from the scullery door Doug was strolling towards us across the sunlit field with the rod apparently undamaged and his landing net bulging. Anglers are the most easy-going, tolerant, likeable people it is possible to imagine; the only thing that upsets them is to see another angler with a net full of fish.

'You're up then, lads?' he said, as if he had only just noticed us and flipped his net over so that nine glittering trout tumbled on to the grass. I'm not good at mathematics but I'd counted them before they touched the ground. They were not sea-trout but it was a excellent bag all the same. They were the wild brown trout of the stony streams, speckled and still wet with the cold hill water. There was a perfectly good cooker on the other side of the door but we made a ring of stones, lit a wood fire and cooked them over the embers in the sunshine. I cannot remember a more perfect breakfast and even the fact that Douglas had caught every one did not seem to matter as we leaned against the sun-warm cottage walls and watched the morning meadows.

Anglers, although manly in every possible way, do nevertheless have a characteristic which reminds me of most females I have known. If my wife is attending a function (or even going next door to a casual drinks party) she feels that a new dress would be appropriate or even vital to the success of the occasion. I don't say that she always gets one but, if she does, it is never quite right with the shoes she intended to wear. If new shoes also are obtained, by skilful argument, I know that they will not look right with the only handbag she is prepared to be seen dead with. I think I need not go on. Every male has known *some* female, so every man will know the spiral toward penury which I have in mind. Anglers are a bit like that. A trip to a new river or lake means re-equipping with a host of new baubles which they believe (or have heard) are vital to success. Their collection of fly boxes, lined with ranks of pretty feathered confections, are discarded as being useless at that particular venue

(as if they were ever much use at any other). If they can hide the fact from their wives they are quite likely to invest in a new rod or reel with, of course, the right weight of floating line to go with it or even a pair of the kind of waders that a man dare not be without on that water. At the very least they will fill several boxes with the kind of salmon or trout flies that will suggest considerable knowledge of local conditions.

The rivers of the West Country tend to wend their way not only through some of the most attractive scenery in Britain but, also, through some of the narrowest, rockiest, tree-hung fairy glens one can imagine. It was obviously stupid of me to buy a river if I was not prepared to purchase also the equipment which was needed to fish it. I had, therefore, obtained the bare necessities, like a selection of each of the flies recommended by the local fishing emporiums and a tasteful camouflaged jacket with eleven pockets and a zip-on storm hood; a pair of the only waders to be recommended for wading on West Country rocks and a delightful brook rod. The rod was only six feet long when assembled and almost weightless. My other fly reels were far too heavy for it, of course, and it would have been useless without the beautifully engineered, almost jewel-like, reel that went with it.

The manufacturers also thought of their product as jewellery judging by the price but, after all, it was no use spoiling the ship for a ha'porth of tar. That rod was built for fishing in fairy glens and when a man has a fairy glen or two of his own, what else can he do?

The mill pool was deep and placid except where it poured over the edge of the dam and cascaded down among the mossy boulders below so it was not possible to step off the bank there. But when the white water had ceased its roar and settled down to a gentler music as it flowed on from pool to glassy pool, it could be fished only by wading in thigh-boots. We waded then, that summer day, all three after our breakfast by the sunny wall, but far apart for safety's sake and to avoid disturbing each other's water. The river beat was not half a mile in length but I did not see my companions for several hours. There were open banks here and there where nervous sheep looked down from the fields above, bleated in panic and disappeared about their business. Fiery red bullocks, too, appeared from time to time, snorting and jostling each other for a better view then turning upon each other, skull to skull, and struggling for supremacy like shaggy giants at a tournament, until small avalanches of dust and stones tumbled down the bank into the water.

There were hundreds of small trout among the boulders. Hardly a rock that did not shelter a fish behind its bulk. No sleek, well-fed beauties these, like their brothers in the food-rich, gentler waters of the Test, but lively glittering creatures, flashing like jewels in their endless struggle to hold station in the fast runnels of water and catch their share of food. There were few places on the rocky bed of this river where weeds could take firm hold or insects gather in great numbers. Sometimes, when little rain had fallen on the moors for weeks, dark patches of water weed appeared in sheltered spots, but when the rain clouds gathered on the hills and thunder rolled, the rocky bed was gouged out clean of vegetation by the raging torrents that tore through its canyons to the sea.

No matter that the river bed and any minerals which might be lurking beneath it belonged, according to my deeds, to the Duchy of Cornwall, the air was no less sweet for that nor the heron, hunched beneath the alders, no less pessimistic as he surveyed the water from one skinny leg. But the dipper on the wet rocks bobbed and bowed and curtsied as if he were expecting the Duke at any moment.

A few hundred yards of this kind of fishing could keep a man happy through a long summer day. Each separate pool was like a new country to explore. Each boulder was a fresh challenge in the fascinating game of trying to drop a weightless fly, like falling gossamer, a few feet upstream of each rock so that it would sweep down the right thread of moving water, hurry round the stone and be caught for a brief moment in the back eddy where the fish was waiting. They would strike like lightning if all was right and reaction in a split second was vital to have any chance of catching him. Perhaps only once in four or five casts would the lure touch the surface on the right spot and even then the quarry was usually too quick for me. There were other hazards, too, to overcome. An inch too far across the boulder's upstream bulge would carry the tiny scrap of feather down the wrong side and wrap the filament, fine as a spider might extrude, around the stone. And even when one's judgement seemed just right and the lure moved swiftly round close to the smooth side of the rock, it sometimes moved a millimetre left or right and caught up in a strand of clinging moss. And there it would hold like a miniature anchor until the current's pressure on the looping line would tear it free and hurl it down the stream – a dark blob of wet moss which no self-respecting trout would deign to notice.

These trout, or most of them, were far too tiny to take from the river. Time and again I would dip my left hand in the cold water and hold one on my palm, glittering and wriggling like an animated brooch for perhaps two seconds before it flicked back to its own familiar world. It is a cliche that most hunters respect their quarry, even love it, and it's true. No gentle Bambi, licking the face of some self-satisfied naturalist on the glossy cover of a book, can move me like a wild brook trout or a flight of geese across the moon. They care nothing for the human race that degrades them by its interference.

Some of the glassy-surfaced pools were wide and often deep, especially where the water was enclosed by steep rocks and giant tumbled boulders. Each crack and crevice was hung about with a rich profusion of ferns and mosses, and the convoluted roots of the overhanging trees made textured patterns on the river bank. The roots provided hand holes, too, where deep water made me take the utmost care. The water in these basins was calm except along their outer edges and the trout could relax their struggle with the tireless current. Perhaps because of this release from endless energy expenditure they tended to be larger here and rose to ring the placid surface in less haste. I had two trout of several ounces from one pool and, although I let them go again, they were the giants of the day which I prized more highly than many a fat, stew-fed rainbow of as many pounds which sometimes fell to my fly on richer rivers further east. But even these fish in the quiet basins were not easy to deceive. It was difficult in places to find a firm foothold far enough away from the high banks to roll the fly line back and forth without repeated snagging on some dipping twig or sprouting clump of ferns. In quiet water, too, the trout had time to watch the offered lure, to see its man-made, clumsy dressing or the line of light along the filament which held it. They were more inclined to let the fly drift by knowing that it was not food. Their brothers in the fast runnels had but a fraction of a second to decide such matters and had to snatch at any morsel that came by before it disappeared forever from their little world of scarcity.

I cannot bring myself to believe, as some fishermen do, that fish become so educated that they know they are being angled for. No doubt when they have once engaged their jaws on an angler's hook and lived they tend to be more careful in their choice of tempting morsels and so become more difficult to catch. Their instinct, too, will force them to react cautiously when a human figure moves within their sky-lit window or vibrates the river banks with clumsy steps. But I cannot believe that they connect the fisherman's fly along a continuous thread of nylon and floating line to the figure on the bank. It can hardly ever be possible for a fish to see the whole chain from lure to angler in relatively shallow flowing water, much less to understand that one controls the other. I cannot but think that some fish are more wary than others from the start and thus their chances of survival are that much greater.

And yet, after years of careful observation, I know nothing of their mystery. That day in an area of fast water over a gravel bed I looked behind me and saw two trout each using one of my legs as protective boulders, scarce three inches away from the green rubber of my waders. When I moved a pace or two they followed. Were they mad? Had they no instinct for survival? Or was it simply that my clumsy feet disturbed the water creatures from the gravel bed and provided a cornucopia of sustaining food? It may be so, for river fish will often gather in large numbers downstream of shallow water where the cattle drink.

We met again below the tumbling water of the dam and only Bob had caught a fish worth taking back to supplement the larder. We sat there for a while upon a rock and talked of our adventures like a group of warriors returned from far-off battles. We told of devil trees that snagged our back casts in their knotted fingers, of rocky ledges where we almost came to grief and little fish like Sirens, tempting us to take another and another step into the enchanted pools. Bob hid his modest fish inside his bag in case we should meet some stranger on the way. 'Any luck, gentlemen?'

'No! Nothing rising, I'm afraid.'

And we walked back across the meadows to the mill.

We never did catch a trout of more than a few ounces at Penruin and we never caught one of the sea-trout either, but it made not one jot of difference to the pleasure of those golden days. The last night we sat in the riverside pub talking to the locals, one asked us if we had caught any sea-trout, although we were quite sure he knew we hadn't.

'No,' we said. 'They've never taken the slightest notice of anything we offered them.'

'Nay midears,' he said. 'You'm 'ave to know 'em a bit to catch they.'

And he was right. When we opened the cottage door the next morning there was a parcel wrapped in newspaper. It contained three brace of fine sea-trout. Someone obviously knew a bit about they . . . and we knew a bit about where they came from.

The Silent Voices

I am in no way psychic, nor have I ever had a mystical experience of any kind and, although I like to think that I keep an open mind on all subjects, I must confess to being sceptical about such matters. Of one thing I am sure, however; buildings often have an atmosphere about them which is almost palpable. Some houses are happy places, some are sad and a few hold an inexplicable aura of menace which is disturbing. I have been in big, rambling houses where empty rôoms and bare staircases have cried welcome and pretty cottages where the very air was melancholy.

Cornwall has always been a unique county to me, not only because its rocky coastline, its fishing ports and villages and its wild moorland are quite different from those in any other part of Britain, but because it has an atmosphere – an almost physical feeling in the air – of strange and ancient mystery. It pervades the whole area from the Tamar River to Land's End and I have never experienced quite the same thing anywhere else. I have often tried to analyse it but it defies mere logic. Its presence is too close to ignore, too powerful to defy. It is a land of legend where myth is more powerful than fact. I think it all has something to do with the rocks.

In spite of jagged crags and boiling sea, of wreckers, pirates, smugglers and disaster, the coastline can relax and smile, and often does, but the solid core of the ancient kingdom lies like a sleeping animal, ignoring the flies that crawl upon its hide, and waits, breathing gently and knowing all. The stone hedges and the cottages, the churches and the manor houses are chips off the old rock and belong where they are and nowhere else. They share the power, the rugged beauty, the vague menace.

The names are as unique as the rocks and hold the same mystery and magnetism. Marazion, Madron and Morrah, Perranzabulo and Pendrift, Legant, Restormel, Demelza and Lyonesse. Like a list of heroes from some romantic saga. And what man journeying to

Indian Queens would not think himself upon the road to Samarkand?

Penruin was Cornish and made of Cornish rock like the stone circles and the moorland cairns. It was itself megalithic with its outhouses strewn about it like fallen pieces crumbling back to shale.

It held the same strange atmosphere which I could never quite fathom. It drew me like a magnet and yet at point of contact it held aloof waiting for a sign or password which I did not know. I owned it but it would not be possessed. It held on always to some faint echo of the past of the people who built it and worked it through the years. This feeling manifested itself most strongly in the yard on sunny afternoons when the warm air was alive with half-heard sounds and voices.

No ghostly apparitions, these, stalking the shadowy rooms. The noises of the night were only the scratching of some questing mouse, the cistern dripping in the cobwebbed mill or the gentle rubbing on the cottage walls of some wakeful sheep finding relief from fly-blown irritation beneath its fleece. Even the sudden rattle of the cowshed door was just a bullock scratching. There were some nights when we first slept at Penruin when we felt a strange unease that kept us wakeful. The scratching was too loud and the timbers cracked like giant knuckles flexing. On those nights, too, the ram pump in a neighbour's river field became insistent, impinging on the tired mind. It beat a steady rhythm, growing ever louder until it shook the ground, the mill, the very pillow like the pounding heartbeat of the sleeping valley. But soon these noises became familiar and we hardly heard them any more.

No, the ghosts at Penruin were no disturbing phantoms of the night but the echoes of those who went about their daily work there in the yard through the long years. Sounds there were which I could hear and yet not quite hear. On dull or wet days there seemed no-one there but ourselves and the mill withdrew into itself, morose and sulky. But when I was alone in the sun-warm angle of the yard and the birds were busy again along the gutters, the voices were all about me.

They called from within the mill, shouting above the clatter and rumble of the spinning wheels. The miller's wife was busy in the cottage or hanging out her washing in the orchard where the hens scratched among the primroses or fallen apples, or gathered cackling around the granite feeding troughs. They were still there, the troughs, the ruined hen-coops, the rusty milk churns and the clothes prop, leaning against the trunk of a twisted apple tree. The hub and spokes of a big cartwheel lay in the nettles against the dilapidated chicken house. Soft as balsa wood it was, processed by time and weather, and pale as the dry bones of some long-dead animal. One curving segment of the wooden wheel was held in space upon a withered spoke, a geometric remnant unstung by the hypodermic nettle hairs that brushed against it in the breeze. The rest had fallen one by one like mellow apples and lay half buried where they fell across the rusty iron of the rim. How many years had passed, I wondered, since it had spun – bright as a twirling parasol upon the miller's cart when it was new?

In the early days the corn for the mill would have been delivered by a team of heavy horses pulling one of those beautiful ship-like wagons. The path from the lane above was steep and narrow and paved with stones of granite, smooth and slippery. It must have been a difficult operation bringing a heavy load down that slope. Even with the brakes hard on the horses would have been lathered with the strain of holding the cart in check. I could swear I heard the rumble of the wheels and clash of iron hooves pawing the slithering stones for grip. What a turmoil there must have been in the yard when the wagon reached the mill and unloading began. I could hear the miller's wife complaining when the children left the cottage door ajar so that dust swirled in.

Although Penruin had long ceased to grind corn when we first came upon it, the dust and last year's skeleton leaves still swirled about the yard in a miniature whirlwind when quite gentle breezes blew and there were but three or four paces between the cottage door and the mill. Marks upon the granite wall showed clearly that a porch had once protected it and, although I never saw my mill when it was working, even the traditional nick-name 'Dusty Miller' suggests that dust was a great nuisance if not a professional hazard for both the miller and his wife.

There must have been children at Penruin too at some time. I found a child's ball of thin red rubber, deep in the rotting twigs and leafmould below the matted hedge. Its side was ripped and the nest of grass within suggested that it had already been discovered by some opportunist mouse or vole. There was a toy wheel, long rusted in the mouldy straw of the disused chickenhouse, which had once been part of an infant's tricycle and I came upon a large glass marble among the pebbles in the millrace; 'glaggies' we called them when I was a child in Cheshire, and I held it up to the light and wondered again at the bright rainbow of swirls and spirals. I wondered who had found those just like it which I had lost so long ago and whether they also peered into them, twirling them slowly near their eyes and delighting in the warm, noisy fairground of light and colour which they hold forever inside their smooth crystal.

The mill, the cottage and the cow byre were all joined together to form a single irregular-shaped building and although they each had their own individual characters, they shared the common feeling of sudden abandonment and withdrawal into the past. The pig room below the cottage staircase was the most forbidding part of the entire structure when we first explored it. But it was also the smallest room and was that much easier to deal with, at least as far as clearing it was concerned. It was not much bigger than a large cupboard because the stair-well occupied about a third of the entire width and the triangular space below it was filled by the great rough stone bath. The slabs of Delabole slate which lay along the opposite wall did not improve the general feeling in the room but it was undoubtedly the hooks driven into the low ceiling beams which gave it the final touch of horror.

It was a simple cell for butchery, practical in its day no doubt, and probably necessary to anyone who kept his own pig, which was a common country practice. From time to time in past years it must have been a cornucopia of good things for the whole family and it is doubtful whether it would have been any more unpleasant in their eyes than the fridge or freezer is today. It is a safe bet that the food which came from it tasted much better. However that might be, we were glad to see the bath outside in the yard where it looked quite innocuous – attractive even, and the cold stone slabs and sharp hooks were not mourned when they departed.

It became a small, pretty spare bedroom and the little window which looked towards the river had great charm and character. Everyone who used it said so and they were right. All the same, within the family it was always called the pig room and we had to be most careful not to refer to it as such when friends were occupying it; it would have been difficult to explain such a faux pas to guests one way or the other, especially if they snored a lot.

The small sittingroom was the friendliest and most relaxing part of the cottage. When the sagging ceiling was removed by Mr Pretty's men to expose the original beams, it was discovered that they had been almost entirely eaten away, presumably by rats. It is not surprising that rats are attracted to a mill but why they should wish to spend so much of their time gnawing away at wood when there must always have been a fair amount of grain about is a mystery. Every beam had to be replaced with new timber. Otherwise, once the dreadful paintwork on the door had been cleaned off and the work done properly, the place was most attractive. It was a small room, dominated by an almost elegant window of small panes which looked across the pasture towards the river and the sloping fields beyond. There was a deep windowseat below and panelled shutters on either side. The original stone fireplace had been uncovered and it was flanked by pretty glass-fronted cupboards where the miller's wife must have kept her best china long ago. This was the easiest room to keep warm being small and cosy, and luckily the fireplace did not smoke. We tended to gather there on winter evenings and we liked it. Sometimes we even felt that it liked us.

The bigger livingroom at the other end of the hallway was handsome rather than pretty when it was finished. We installed an immense new central beam as a firm foundation for the rebuilt ceiling and added a few more smaller cross beams to the original sparse supports. It was strong then and it looked it, the kind of ceiling the walls deserved, built as they were like a castle keep. The coffin chute, for that I'm sure is what it was, that big square hole cut in the ceiling which kept us wondering, had gone and it was difficult to imagine that it had ever existed. In cold weather the room was not easy to keep warm, but it had its moments in the long summer days, when the window and the front door in the hallway beyond were open to the suntrap of the mill yard. It could be a cool haven then with the sounds and smells of the countryside drifting in. It had a character as strong as its walls, that slate-flagged room, and it was never much impressed by folk from up country.

The scullery didn't care. It was too low down the social scale for that. It seemed as old as the rest of the building but it was an afterthought, built on to the side of the main edifice in lean-to fashion so that, if the rest had moved away, it would have fallen down. It was not only unpretentious, it was cheerful. After all, when the sun rose above the valley side each morning, which was the first room to feel its drowsy warmth? It had a red-tiled floor – not up to genuine Delabole slate of course, but it did not care. It had a tap. *Two* taps when we overcame Mr Pretty's resistance, and a good deep white sink and even an electric power point. The rest of the cottage could think what it liked, the scullery was not bigoted. It didn't mind that we were not millers or even that we were not Cornish. It liked us and we liked it and we leaned against its door jamb and didn't have to put on airs.

As we did so we were only a few paces away from the door of the cowshed which was cut into the main wall to our right. The wooden door had slots pierced through it, presumably to let in air. It seemed an unnecessary extravagance because there was another ill-fitting door directly opposite which opened into the kitchen garden, and that let in enough draughts for any reasonable fresh air fiend, human, animal or otherwise.

I could never quite make up my mind about the cow byre. It had only two standings and one tiny window high up in the apex of the gable end. Come to think of it (which I should have done a long time ago) those slots in the wooden door were probably intended to let in more light rather than fresh air. With a hundred years of dirt on the inaccessible six-inch by nine-inch window it would have been difficult to locate a cow's udder on a cold, dark morning with both doors shut. What I could not quite make up my mind about was its character, not its appearance. It was a muck-heap, both at ground level and up on the half floor which passed for a hayloft. There were piles of things up there which I was in no hurry to pick over. It was fairly thick with the atmosphere of Penruin as well as with dirt and rubbish and yet its threat was mere posturing; it was too scruffy to be taken seriously.

Round the door which led out to the pasture the stone wall had been painted with a broad band of white. It was a neater job than the workmen did on the sittingroom door at their first attempt, although it had obviously been there for a long time. I have seen doorways treated in the same way on several farms and I understand that it is intended to guide the cows so that they will find the opening and not walk straight into the solid wall. I have seen a lot of cows going into cowsheds in my time and have never seen one miss the target yet, but I have never watched them doing in it pitch darkness and have often walked into walls myself in those conditions, so I expect the white line had its uses.

I moved a fair amount of rubbish out of the building on the night we lit our first fire and almost choked to death, but I had barely scratched the surface. I finally tackled the job with both doors wide open on a bright sunny morning and, like so many nasty things in the woodshed, it wasn't too bad once one faced up to it. In fact, it was quite interesting. I didn't trust the hayloft and dragged the old sacks and straw and mouldy clothing off the edge with a rake head fixed to a long pole. When I could see more of the wooden flooring it turned out to be remarkably solid and I was able to walk about on it with reasonable confidence and even brush it down with a yard brush. I expected to disturb some rats up there but found none and, what is more remarkable, in spite of nocturnal scratchings, I never saw a rat the whole time we were at Penruin, either indoors or out, and I didn't see so much as a mouse inside the buildings.

When the whole place was cleared, the rubbish burned and the dust had settled, I was able to examine my finds. There was a Victorian bedstead of ornate black iron with brass top rail and fittings. Both ends were there but a brass knob was missing and only one castor had survived. My mother had one like it when I was an infant but most of the examples I had seen were used to plug gaps in hedges on the farms I knew in Cheshire, and very nice they looked. As the Victorian bedstead supplies ran out they tended to be replaced by pieces of corrugated iron. When these were red and rusty they made wonderful splashes of colour in paintings of farmscapes, but they never had the linear quality of the old bedsteads. It's all barbed wire now. The art of plugging hedges is a thing of the past.

I came across a pair of old gaiters of the kind which countrymen wore before the gumboot age. Something or other had been eating those from time to time; it may have been the same mouse that had made its nest in the padding of the horse-collar in the corner of the loft, although he didn't appear to have been at home for some time. There was a rusty horseshoe from a heavy draught horse, a giant compared to the light and shapely one nailed above the door, and some small remnants of trace harness. I brushed everything well and left each object hanging on the walls, including some lengths of chain.

There were a few old pictures which had been discarded at some time from the cottage. The frames were textured with woodworm and the glass was broken. They were all large sepia photographs. One was of a man of indeterminate age with moustache and side whiskers; he was standing proudly erect but unsmiling and holding the head of a big horse with a ribbon at the forelock. Another was of a lady with a simple white bonnet standing, encased in dark clothing from neck to foot; she was by a small wicket gate and was as unsmiling as the man with the horse. There were two vague portraits, oval in shape, and as uncompromising in demeanour as the rest. There was no clue as to who they might have been, those dignified folk, and the yellowed cardboard was badly damaged by mice and damp in every case. There seemed no visible connection with Penruin and no reason to suppose that they had ever lived there.

The only other object of any real interest was a piece of timber fitted with cast iron brackets which held a metal spindle along its length. The wood was recessed to allow a heavy iron cog to turn freely in the centre. It was part of the control mechanism of a sluice-gate and I took it across to the mill and stored it with a collection of similar artefacts, of which there were many.

The cow byre was at the southern end of Penruin and it was my intention to convert it later to a single livingroom with a small bedroom above. It would have been sunnier than the existing living quarters and with a pleasant view, and it could have been done without destroying any of the building's character. I made a lot of drawings of how I wanted it to look and after lengthy discussions with Don Chambers, he converted my sketches into working drawings. The final plans were approved by the local authority. I made my own designs for a trout lake in the meadow which would have been fed by the mill leat. When the river authority withdrew its alarming suggestion of charging me for the use of the water, I submitted that scheme also and permission to proceed was given. Unfortunately I never carried these projects out because we did not live there long enough but, although I have made a similar pool at my present home, I would dearly have liked to see Penruin reflected in the broad waters of a lake.

The mill yard, apart from the main path from the lane, was very rough indeed. It was bordered on the north and western side by outbuildings which could only be described as ramshackle. The slate roofs had disintegrated in some places and the northern line was almost completely roofed in corrugated iron, much of which was red with rust. Wooden doors, bare of any traces of paint, were deeply fissured and grained by long exposure to sunshine and rain, and hung loosely on metal hinges in the last stages of fatigue.

A small stream trickled through a gutter almost two feet wide and eighteen inches deep which was formed of rude slabs of stone. It

was the sort of duct which one might expect to be uncovered during
an archaeological dig on the site of some ancient settlement. The rest
of the area was paved, if that is the correct word, by similar stones

scattered about as if dropped by a melting glacier at the end of the
Ice Age. Docks, nettles, grass and a profusion of weeds grew lustily
in every crevice and any attempt to traverse the ground was made
more hazardous by disintegrating chicken coops, rusty milkchurns,
odds and ends of cast iron, broken ladders and the like.

It was exciting and beautiful beyond words. I was forced to
assume that horses and wagons must have used this area to turn
round when they had business at the mill but, although here and
there a flattish piece of rock had been used to bridge the channel
through which the streamlet ran, I could not conceive what kind of
horses could manoeuvre a heavy vehicle across such difficult
terrain. Turning the car was hazardous enough when only a foot or
two of this ground was needed to achieve the necessary lock on the
wheels and I was glad I never had to do it without someone behind
to warn me when I was in danger of losing the exhaust system.

That piece of yard with its ragged fringe of tumble-down buildings was one of those problems to which there is no completely satisfactory answer. On the one hand it could not be ignored because in a few years time the whole place would have fallen into heaps of rubble. Even if it had been possible to save the buildings and smarten them up, it would not have been possible to do so without destroying, or at best changing, their character. If the whole yard could have been relaid using the original stones it would certainly have become both useful and attractive; the dilemma of the little brook, however, would have been almost insoluble. It cut the width of the yard in half, but the thought of driving it underground was not to be borne and the use of asphalt or even gravel would have been a heresy. As things turned out I never had to solve the problem for we were not there long enough and I still remember it as a beautiful shambles.

Two of the doorways had been outlined in white like the cow byre so animals must have been kept there, but one of these was blocked halfway up its height by a huge and rather random block of cement. I could not imagine the purpose of that. There was plenty of evidence inside that one part had been used as a stable. There was a wooden manger still clinging to the mouldering wall and I came across a heavy lump of rounded wood with a large hole through the centre, like a giant bead. It was a sinker, a wooden weight which had once been at the bottom end of a rope which was tied at the top to a horse's headstall. The rope passed through a ring on the side of the manger and the sinker ensured that the rope did not become tangled when the horse moved its head about.

There was a nosebag too, or what remained of one, hanging on a rusty nail. It was made of woven matting with leather corners and it reminded me vividly of my own childhood. Although I lived in a town there were still a few horse-drawn vehicles about. A big black shire with white feather on his front legs delivered salt in huge blocks to a nearby fishmonger's shop. It was a very leisurely business. The carter would find out what supplies old Eddie Martin needed and would return to the cart, roll back the green tarpaulin that protected his cargo and saw flat slabs of salt from the blocks. These he would then subdivide into handy pieces about the size of a house brick and carry them into the shop. The salt man would sit and chat whilst Eddie wrapped the slabs in newspaper squares ready to sell for a penny per block. They would puff away at their Woodbines and laugh extravagantly at remarks which I could never understand. No! The salt man smoked the Woodbines which he got at five for tuppence from a slot machine in the doorway of the milk-shop next door; Eddie smoked Greys' cigarettes – I'm sure of that because he gave me the little, rather flattened lead soldiers which were given away in each packet.

Meanwhile, I would stand on the edge of the pavement by the horse's head and look up at him. He was as big as a dinosaur and not unlike one with his head buried in the nosebag. The salt man put the nosebag on the horse as soon as they came to a halt outside the shop. It kept the animal quiet during the long wait he always had. I would move along and watch the saltman sawing the blocks and wish I could earn my living one day doing a fantastic job like that, but he would never let me have a go. 'I've seen kids saw their bloody 'eads off trying to do this,' he would say. I would follow him into the shop and stand by the counter listening to his conversations with Eddie. Eddie never cared how long I spent following him about but the salt man used to get a bit irritated. 'Go an see if me 'orse 'as buggered off, son,' he would say and out I would go to look, although we could all see him well enough through the shop window.

'He's still there, Mister,' I'd report.

'Right, son, keep an eye on 'im for me will yer?' he'd say, and out I would go and stand under the horse's nose, keeping an eye on him. The salt man never adjusted the nosebag strap so that the horse was always in difficulties trying to reach some more bait. He would try to get at it by pressing it against the ground but his collar and harness made it difficult so he would throw his head up in the air and a cloud of chaff would explode over his head. It went up his nostrils as well as into his eyes and he would snort violently into the bag to get it out, sending up more clouds of chaff and dust which got into my eyes too. My face would get streaked with tears and dust through trying to get it out.

When the salt man took the nosebag off before departing he

would always give the horse's head a rub down with his hand, stroke his muzzle and give his neck a few loud slaps. ''E keeps gettin chaff in 'is eyes,' he'd say, looking down at me, 'silly old sod!'

I would watch them rumble away, knowing exactly how the old horse felt.

I left the nosebag on the rusty nail at Penruin (it looked very fragile) and moved on into the calf pen nextdoor. The floor was of tightly packed dung and straw, there was a granite trough, a metal bucket and another old milkchurn. Rain coming in through the shattered roof was the only thing that had moved in there for a very long time.

The last compartment was where the miller had kept his pig or pigs; there was no doubt of that for the opening in the wall was hardly more than three feet high. There were heavy granite troughs inside and outside among the nettles, signs that there had once been a small enclosure where the animals could move freely in and out. It was dry in that section but apart from the drone of bluebottles it slept as soundly as the rest. The world those buildings knew had gone forever and they were content to drowse in the sunshine and wait for the end like tired old men.

The sluicegate and waterwheel occupied the space between the outbuildings and the mill wall and, when we first saw it, a heavy angle iron had been thrust through the main window of the grinding floor so that it had not only smashed the glass but had shattered the framework also, pushing the whole assembly outwards at the bottom. The iron still lay where it had fallen, half in and half out of the opening.

It was the only sign of vandalism, however. There were some minor cracks in the massive walls and several of the brick arches above the doors and windows needed attention, but these were clearly caused by vibration and the lapse of time. Unlike the crumbling outhouses, the mill showed not the slightest sign of giving in. It was waiting quietly like the rest of Penruin but certainly not for the end.

As soon as the cottage was habitable the arches of the mill were repaired, the cracks dealt with and the windows replaced with new ones of the same design.

I had always loved water-mills, probably because I had been fascinated since early childhood by anything concerned with water, but I knew very little about how they worked or what life was like for a miller and his family. Bob had been in the milling trade for many years before he had taken up farming in Hampshire, but I did not realize how strongly the profession was still in his blood.

Many mornings when he was staying at Penruin on our fishing trips Bob would be up at dawn wandering about the buildings. The mill was small but was an endless source of interest and fascination to him. We spent many hours exploring and unravelling the technical mysteries of man's first industrial machine. Objects which meant little or nothing to me then held all the joy of treasure trove for Bob and soon I was as engrossed as he in trying to understand it all. A heavy wooden club, pitted by woodworm, which lay in a dusty corner he recognized as the handle – or thrift – of a stone dresser's bill. This was the tool used to carve the ridges, or furrows, on the surface of the millstones and we found several of the metal blades too after a short search. These heavy steel objects were like elongated lozenges, forming a double-ended chisel and they were fitted into a square hole at the top of the handle where they were retained by wedges. Other simple triangles of heavy wood were identified as the wedges used to support the millstones when they were being moved, or dressed. At the stage when we began to explore seriously, such work as we had persuaded Mr Pretty to do had been concentrated on the cottage. The interior of the mill was still untouched and was for that reason more interesting to examine. The jumble of cogs, wheels, pulleys, belts, chains and general rubbish which occupied each floor was still to be sorted and identified and, if possible, the pieces returned to their original places. With Bob's guidance and some study on my own account the jigsaw puzzle began to take shape. I was surprised to discover on what simple principles this complicated mechanism worked.

It was not unlike the little clockwork toys we wound up as children, if one substituted the power of the turning waterwheel for the coiled spring and the rotating millstones for the spinning wheels of our toy engines. I made some little diagrammatic drawings to clarify the system in my own mind. Once I had grasped the main principles I was able to understand the detail also, to identify a small cog or stone roller which lay near a field gate or in the brambles of the river field. It was a great joy to recognize such pieces and return them to the mill. The bulk of the heavy machinery, the large wheels and gears and the millstones in their wooden cases, were still in place, as was a good deal of the drive mechanism in the upper floor, which provided take-off power for the sack hoist and other ancillary machinery.

Bob was carried away by his enthusiasm and I was pulled willingly along with him. He would find a strange piece of metal in an old drawer full of apparent rubbish. 'Look!' he would say, 'that's a damsel.' It looked nothing like a damsel to me, but I didn't argue. 'See?' he exclaimed, 'that should be attached to the vertical drive shaft in the eye of the upper, running millstone. No, not the bed stone. That doesn't move. Look! Just below the grain hopper there's that wooden shoe that feeds the corn into the eye of the revolving stone. See? Well, everything is going along fine and the miller hears his wife call "Tea up" or "scrumpy up" and off he goes to have five minutes while the mill grinds away. Now, how does he know that the grain won't jam up in that shoe bit and stop flowing? Simple! He's got his damsel, hasn't he? See, it spins round on the spindle and keeps jogging the shoe to make sure there's a steady flow of grain to the stones. A grain blockage could be very serious but if the damsel fails him he's always got his "warbler". Millers weren't just pretty faces, you know. You thought that bit of string was just a big of string, didn't you? Well, it's not; that worked his warbler. See, on one end was a bit of leather (that dried-up bit in the box there is probably it) which he put inside the hopper with the grain on top. The grain held it in position by its weight and the string was attached at the other end to his warbler alarm. If the weight of the grain became too light the leather shifted out of position and that bit of string, as you call it, set off his warbler and it was panic-stations.'

I began to appreciate that a miller in the old days had plenty to occupy his mind. It came as a revelation to me to learn that when a mill was not being used it had to be put out of gear, like a modern car. Bob pointed out two small cog wheels which would mesh with a much larger one when the mill was running. They were called

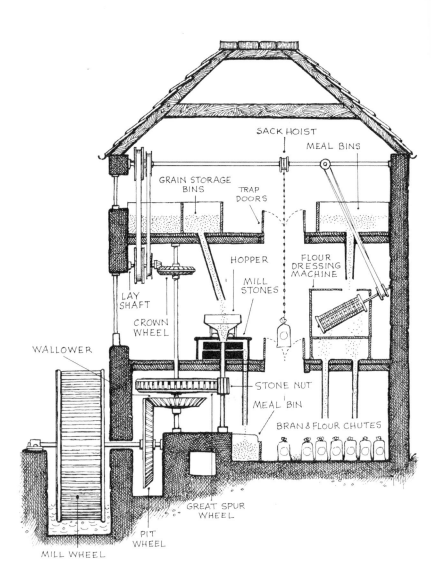

SACK HOIST

MEAL BINS

GRAIN STORAGE
BINS

TRAP
DOORS

HOPPER

FLOUR
DRESSING
MACHINE

MILL
STONES

LAY
SHAFT

CROWN
WHEEL

WALLOWER

STONE NUT

MEAL BIN

BRAN & FLOUR CHUTES

GREAT SPUR
WHEEL

PIT
WHEEL

MILL WHEEL

'stone nuts', he said, and were normally the only cogs which it was possible to lift out of gear. It was very important that this should be done at the end of the day, he explained, for in the event of a heavy and unexpected rainstorm during the night the mill leat or pond might overflow or the sluice gate be carried away by the weight of water. In such an event the wheel would start to turn and the unattended machinery would run wild and unchecked to almost certain disaster.

In the eighteenth century cast iron was introduced into mills and must have simplified many of the engineering problems associated with the old wooden machinery, excellent though it was. It would no doubt have been very expensive to convert from wood to iron all at one time, so it tended to be introduced here and there as the need arose. Penruin was, even then, still in a hybrid stage. The spokes of the wheel were of wood, as were the paddles, but the rim, hub and axle were metal. Within the mill it had been converted almost completely to cast iron gearing but many of the wheels were still cogged with apple wood teeth which meshed with other wooden teeth or iron ones. The mixture seemed to work very well and it was not difficult to understand that the use of wooden teeth cut down the noise considerably. Some say they lasted just as long.

You will see the principles on which Penruin worked in my diagram on page 144. Most watermills operated on very similar lines but every mill was built as an individual machine to suit the available water supply and the geography of the surrounding countryside. The gravitational power of water was exploited by man from earliest times and has served him for two thousand years and more. The mechanism of early mills was made entirely of wood and it is sobering to contemplate the skill and knowledge of the millwrights who were the mechanical engineers of their time.

The mill-wheel at Penruin was of the breast-shot type, which means that the water supply from the leat made contact with the paddles at about the height of the axle. Undershot wheels were driven by water pushing the paddles from below and over-shot by water falling from above and contacting the wheel forward of its apex, thus turning it in the opposite direction. The axle tree passed through the granite wall of the mill and turned a large, cast-iron pit

wheel which was bevelled and fitted with teeth made of apple wood. The lower half of this large wheel was sunk (as its name implies) into a narrow pit and was cast in two halves so that it could be fitted or removed, if necessary, without the need to dismantle the axle and waterwheel. The pit wheel teeth meshed with the smaller bevelled cog known as the wallower (Mr Pretty's men called it the waller) which turned the main vertical drive shaft. The wallower was much smaller than the pit wheel and so would have turned at about four times the speed of the waterwheel.

Immediately above the wallower was the great spur wheel, the largest gear in the mill. This was not bevelled at the rim but it too was fitted with wooden teeth, some of which, as in the case of the pit wheel, were now broken.

On the opposite sides of this massive wheel were the two relatively small cogs known as stone nuts, which Bob had pointed out to me. (I have shown only one in my diagram for the sake of simplicity.) They had been lifted out of gear but, when the mill was working, they would have been in the right position to mesh with the wooden teeth of the spur wheel and would have been turned by it at high speed. Each stone-nut turned a vertical shaft which passed through the ceiling to the grinding floor above and drove a set of millstones at about thirty times the RPM of the mill-wheel. The upper floors had double trap-doors in their centres through which sacks of grain would have been raised from ground level to be emptied into the storage bins above. The doors would be opened automatically as the sack passed through and would fall back again by gravity.

In spite of his tendency to ramble off into interesting speculation, Bob gave me clear enough descriptions of the day-to-day working of mills like Penruin for, although like all mills it differed in detail, for the most part it followed the general plan. Grain sacks would have been unloaded from the wagons on to the ground floor and raised by the sack hoist to the top floor where they would be emptied into the wooden storage bins. When grinding work began the grain would pass down the wooden chutes into the hoppers which rested on the top of wooden vats or tuns enclosing the millstones. It would then be fed into the central hole in the upper stone and a steady supply ensured by the wooden shoe and the action of Bob's beloved 'damsel'. As the wheat was ground into meal it would pass outwards via the channels on the stones until it fell from the outer edge and down through the chute into the meal bin on the ground floor.

Simple it all seemed but simple it was not. The more I learned about the mill the more amazed I was by the ingenuity which brought it all about. I was surprised to find that only the upper stone revolved and that although the space between it and the stationary bedstone was as thin as paper, it must not touch at any point. To complicate matters further, when stones warmed up during the grinding process the space between them tended to widen, producing unevenly ground flour. This gap had then to be

adjusted to ensure an even texture; the process was known as 'tentering'. Stones were not allowed to run without a steady flow of grain for, in a sense, the seed was like oil and without it the stones would run dry. If they did and they made surface contact, the results could be very serious. At least they would be badly damaged and if not attended to quickly, could generate enough heat to cause fire. It was little wonder that the millers installed alarm systems to warn them if all was not well.

When the grinding process was complete the meal in the bins was so warm that it had to be left for several days to cool down before it could be dressed and graded.

The precision engineering required to produce an efficient and safe grinding system was surprising enough but to achieve it with such apparently clumsy materials was astonishing. The stones could weigh almost a ton and yet to work properly they had to be balanced as exactly as a sports car's wheels. Small sections were often cut away and filled with molten lead to ensure smooth running.

There were many discarded millstones lying about at Penruin. Some were embedded in the paths and in the stone floor of the mill whilst others lay on the grinding floor or in the long grass of the orchard. Some of them were of solid granite and others were made up of wedges of French burr stone, fitted together to make a perfect disc, like sections of wrapped cream cheese in a round cardboard box. The pieces were cemented together and bound like a wagon wheel with a tight metal rim.

Stones made of granite or Derbyshire peak stone were made in one piece and were used for grist, but those made up of burr stone pieces were considered the best for producing flour. One day I tried to move a discarded stone which lay in the orchard beyond the chicken house and was staggered by the weight and consequent difficulty. Even with a stout wooden lever I could not move it more than a few inches, and yet to keep a mill like Penruin running smoothly, it would have been necessary to move them whenever they needed to be dressed.

The top runner stone was usually raised a few inches with a crowbar and the thin end of a stepped wooden wedge was inserted in the gap. The stone was then levered up again and the wedge pushed in another step. This process would continue until the stone was high enough for a rope to be pushed through the hole in the centre and lifted by means of a block and tackle and turned face upwards on the floor.

The pattern of radiating furrows on the surface of millstones was designed to carry the meal away from the centre and expel it round the edges. It was chipped out with sculptoral accuracy by the stone dressers, using crude bills and chisels. It must have been an arduous task, usually carried out by full-time craftsmen who often worked in cramped conditions. It is said that the sparks which flew from the stone when the blade struck forced tiny specks of metal into the dressers' hands and that one could identify an experienced craftsman by asking him to 'show his steel'.

The main drive shaft of the mill continued up into the grinding floor and was capped by another large cog called the crown wheel. This gear turned the lay shaft which was a horizontal spindle fitted with various wheels beautifully made of wood and, although few of the belts were still in place, they had driven various pieces of ancillary machinery on all three floors.

There was a strange gadget against the wall opposite to the mill stones which puzzled me. It was an open-fronted box which had obviously had doors at some time and it contained a cunningly devised wooden framework in the form of a cylinder. It was lined with wire gauze and through the dust and cobwebs it was possible to detect brushes fixed to a central spindle. The large box sat squarely on the floor but the cylinder was set at a steep angle and the axle protruded through the side of the box to a socket on the wall where there was a wooden wheel, obviously designed to turn the central shaft. It didn't puzzle Bob. It was a wire dressing machine, he said, and was used to separate the bran from the flour. When the meal in the storage bins on the floor above was cool enough it would be fed through a chute into the upper end of the cylinder where the revolving brushes would brush it against the gauze. As it moved downwards, the flour would pass through and the bran and middlings would tail out at the lower end.

The fascination of the watermill was not confined by any means to its machinery alone, for all about it lay personal details and possessions which gave clues to the people who made and worked it. Bob and I would sit upon the wooden stone casting or upon a heavy beam and comb each floor for interesting detail. Much that baffled me was clear enough to him and, if it was not, he would worry over it until he found a reason for its existence. That old leather glove, for instance, with split fingers which lay upon the floor curled like a severed hand in the dust. Who owned it? Was it the miller or the man who dressed the stones who left it there one day and never returned to put it on again? A single nail driven into a beam was enough to set Bob's curiousity nagging him. Who put the nail there and for what purpose? And that tiny triangle of tin nailed to the wooden meal bin, what was it for? No busy man, as Bob said, knocks a big nail into a wooden beam without a purpose or takes his tin-snips to a syrup can and nails a triangle to the bin unless he wants to have it there.

The miller must have been a very busy man indeed. Not only was he working in the centre of a dusty, noisy and dangerous machine, but I saw no evidence whatsoever that any attempt had been made to protect him, or anyone else, from the nightmare consequences of an accident. Wheels, gears and spindles must have been spinning round at high speed in all directions when the mill was in full production but I found no protective guards or barriers anywhere nor, as far as I was able to make out, any method of stopping the juggernaut in an emergency. The mill would come to rest only when the water supply was cut off by lowering the sluice gate, for the stone-nuts could only be lifted out of gear when the machinery had stopped.

There was a rail around three sides of the trap door on the upper floor which must have cut down the chances of stepping backwards into oblivion, but no such luxury was provided on the grinding floor, where most of the activity took place.

The whole purpose of the mill was to grind out meal of one kind or another, and in spite of all hazards it was the miller's job to produce the best possible end product. He was, therefore, constantly obliged to feel the flour as it arrived in the bins, to test the quality. It was said that this lifelong habit produced the large spatulate thumb which all millers were reputed to possess. We examined the deserted, enigmatic glove like Holmes and Dr Watson but I cannot swear to the fact that the thumb was larger than the rest of the worn-out fingers, nor that the miller was left-handed and walked with a limp.

On the other hand I was unable from my own investigation to refute the well-known claim that all millers were not only dusty but dishonest and that they took advantage of their huge thumbs by pushing them well down into the measure when selling flour to customers. In any case I was not disposed to argue the fat with Chaucer who referred to the miller's 'thumb of gold'. If the whole business is only a myth, why do country people still refer to the broad flat bullhead (a number of which I came across, camouflaging themselves like mad among the pebbles of the mill leat) as 'miller's thumbs'?

However that might be, the miller's life was unlikely to have been a sinecure. Neither Rhona, Bob nor I could ever shake off the feeling that something had happened at Penruin that brought about a sudden end to all activity. Something, I mean, more instantly traumatic than the change in social and economic circumstances. There was no sign of the kind of tidying up which one might expect when a lifetime's business is being brought to an end. On the contrary, a pair of work boots in the corner of the grinding floor, a well-worn coat, thick with dust, hanging from a bolthead in the upper storey, the glove and small hand tools strewn about in odd places gave the mill a distinctly *'Mary Celeste'* atmosphere and made us speculate the more about departed occupants.

How many working lives had come and gone within those massive walls, we wondered, and would not each man's life have been uniquely interesting? Simple lives, one might think, in that quiet valley, but were they so simple after all? The engineering skill required to build and maintain such a mill was staggering to contemplate. The control of water with rough stone slabs and wooden sluices to bring it to bear upon the right spot on the wheel as and when required was amazing enough. But the construction of the wheel, massively heavy upon its axle tree which carried the movement to the pit wheel within the walls and passed it on through

a series of gears to the millstones, could only be wondered at, particularly when the whole machine was made of wood, as it must have been in early years.

I found myself asking questions continually but rarely could Bob not find a convincing answer. One could imagine horses bringing the load down the steep lane, however difficult, but how could they pull a big wagon with a full load of flour sacks back up that slope?

'Well,' said Bob, 'that building with the dipping roof was obviously a stable once so the miller must have had his own horse. It would be a big shire or Clydesdale I expect, a kind of muscular booster rocket hooked on in front of the main team to overcome the gravitational pull. He would be ejected (or unhooked) at the top of the hill and return to earth in the paddock below when his job was done.' Brilliant; I had to admit it.

'What about the bit of tin nailed to the flour bin then? That's got you worried.'

'Not really,' said Bob. 'It's in exactly the right spot to cut the string which laced up the flour sacks. It saved using a knife or scissors.'

'The big nail then?' I asked. 'What about the big nail?'

'To hang his dusty cap on when he went in to dinner,' said he, 'That's why it's by the door.'

The more time I spent among the mill workings, the more I could appreciate the industrial archaeology that lay about me, and the more I felt I understood the voices that called above the thunder of the silent gears. But the mill itself remained a menhir, a dolmen, a symbolic monument of ancient stones which held within itself forbidding power. No replaced windowframe or reformed arch, no mended door or lick of paint could touch it. Its walls were gripped by the same dark ivy that clasped the crumbling engine houses upon the bleak moors and, like them, it glowered at me or turned away and was indifferent.

The Millstones Round My Neck

During our years at Penruin many people asked me why I bothered to work on an old water-mill when such things had long been obsolete. It was not an easy question to answer because there were many reasons. It was not only my interest in all things concerned with water but a lifelong conviction that anything visually beautiful is worth preserving for that quality alone. There was also the fact that I had a great interest in architecture and had taught the subject for a short time at a college of art. My main concern was with the history and development of church and domestic architecture in Britain, especially in villages and rural areas. I was never an expert on the subject but my enthusiasm far outstripped my knowledge and I was what was known in those days as a sucker for old buildings. There was also a third reason.

I had realized suddenly that the nature of my job as a freelance artist meant that I was free to live anywhere I chose, within reason, in Britain. It was an enviable situation and a difficult problem to solve. We were spoiled for choice. My wife and I spent about five years in the search for an ideal spot. It could have been a frustrating business but in fact it was not. We enjoyed every day (or almost every day) of our many trips to look at possible homes.

In the 1950s the situation was different from that of the present day. At that time there were dilapidated houses, cottages, barns and mansions all over Britain which no-one seemed to want although many of them were very beautiful. The great and terrible 'boom' in the property market was still far off but even then there seemed to be an army of people mounted on roaring bulldozers just waiting for the signal to sweep them away like so much rubbish. What the planners and speculators put in their places was usually out of character with the surroundings, if not downright ugly. I thought then that nobody cared about the piecemeal destruction of our towns and villages. Although the large number of preservation

groups which have sprung up since have proved me wrong, nevertheless it was a period when many thousands of houses and cottages, which would now be prominent in the 'desirable property' columns, were ruthlessly destroyed.

Things were beginning to improve for me at that time. The precarious life of a freelance artist was losing some of its terror but we were by no means financially secure or even well off. It is an astonishing fact, however, that in those days there were hundreds of country cottages on the market for three or four thousand pounds, and four or five thousand could secure a mansion. I know it because I was offered several. There was a snag, of course. Almost without exception they were what the estate agents describe as 'ripe for modernization' which at best meant that indoor facilities, if they existed at all, were primitive and that they were almost certain to be suffering from damp and wet or dry rot somewhere. At the worst they were so ripe that they were ready to fall at any moment.

In spite of this, many of those houses and cottages were rescued not just by people with a lot of money but by those with enough adventurous spirit to expend endless devotion and hard work upon them. The result has been that most of them are now not only comfortable and attractive homes but are in better condition structurally than they have ever been before. As a bonus they are often a delight to look at and their unique design and indigenous quality attracts not only holidaymakers from our own country but countless thousands of overseas visitors who are delighted by them.

I was walking down the High Street of a Suffolk village recently when an American lady stopped in her tracks and, in a voice which could be heard for a hundred yards, said to her husband, 'My *Gad* Henry! Isn't their Lav-en-ham cute?' Henry was quite right when he grunted, 'It sure is a humdinger, honey. It surely is.'

Those days of home-hunting were an adventure and a delight to Rhona and me. We were lucky because we were in no great hurry and the situations which in other circumstances would have been frustrating were always interesting and often wildly comical.

We were shown round a small mansion in Hampshire with extensive grounds surrounded by twelve-foot-high hedges of clipped yew. We protested that we could not afford to pay the wages of the men who would be needed to keep the hedges neat but our protests were brushed aside. The asking price was a mere five thousand six hundred and had we noted the quality of the oak panelling in the hall? Appreciated the unique decorative plaster-work on the ceilings? (the damaged sections could easily be repaired) and 'What about you, darling?' said the man from the estate agents, chucking our infant daughter under the chin, 'Wouldn't *you* like to live here?' She hung her head and retired behind her mother's skirt, thinking he meant the dilapidated conservatory we were standing in at the time. The truth was that the gardener's cottage would have been on the large side for us but it would have been useless to say so.

In those days the agents were determined to show us everything they had on their books, and they had plenty, much of which had been on the books until the ink was beginning to fade and the property beginning to totter. We were swept from manor house to muck-heap, homestead to hovel. There were cottages so over-crowded that we could hardly get in the door and houses so remote that no-one but the birds had been interested in them since before the war.

The owners, when they were present, were as memorable and varied as their homes. Some were aloof and suspicious, others so friendly and hospitable that it was difficult to get away. Some apologized because an ornament was out of place or a picture not quite straight, whilst others boasted outrageously about houses that were a nightmare. We were surprised how many dwellings had been converted from old stables, out houses, smithies and the like.

We found ourselves one day in an odd-looking building in a remote part of Shropshire where a harassed and bedraggled woman was showing us round. From the moment the door had opened our only desire had been to escape but she was a cheerful, kindly soul and insisted on almost pushing us into every slovenly, scruffy corner of her tiny domain. There was hardly a square foot of furniture or floor space which was not piled with papers, clothing, household utensils and other neglected rubbish. We were desperate to get away. Suddenly she turned to us, scraped her hair back from her face and said with genuine enthusiasm, 'I bet you'd never guess it, but this place used to be a pigsty.'

We were looking at an old barn once (heaven knows why) which was advertised as ideal for conversion to a studio residence. There was not a scrap of wood in it which had not been set upon by rats. The rather pompous farmer who owned it said that he would be glad if we would make up our minds quickly as plenty of other people were nibbling.

We quickly reached a stage where vast numbers of estate agents' pamphlets and other blurb came pouring through our letterbox from all parts of Britain. The details expressed the disorganized state of values at that time. One morning in 1955 or thereabouts we received details of two widely different properties. One was a two-bedroomed cottage in Cookham Dean on the Thames, the other was a castle on the Isle of Wight.

Now it happened, by chance, that a little over ten years before I had been a more or less useless private soldier in the East Yorkshire Regiment and our whole battalion had been billeted in that very castle. I had sat many times upon the highest turret with a Bren gun, a pair of binoculars and a notebook (but no ammunition) with orders to keep an eye on enemy aircraft crossing the coast. (I have noticed that people who are in the way are often asked to keep an eye on things like horses or enemy aircraft.) I don't recall seeing any German planes when I was actually looking for them but I made a lot of sketchbook drawings of distant Portsmouth, the castle, the cookhouse and other oddments.

Another thing I remember about Norris Castle (we used to pop nextdoor to Osborne House to have a bath) is that we had a lot of trouble with ATS girls who used to wait for us in the blackout as we disembarked from the chain ferry across the Medina on Saturday nights. There was nothing romantic about it; they used to wait in doorways and come out screaming like banshees and duff us up. So I remembered that castle vividly . . . And here I was, being offered the entire shooting match for a few hundred pounds less than I was invited to pay for the two-bedroomed cottage at Cookham Dean.

'Let's buy it,' said my wife, and I have admired her for that simple statement ever since. 'We could probably borrow enough if we also scraped the bottom of our own barrel,' she said. 'It would be fun to live in a castle even if we could only occupy one room.' It would have been, I'm sure, but I didn't have her courage. I kept thinking of what we would do if the tower collapsed with dry rot or the roof fell in due to deathwatch beetle. The truth is that my own adventurous spirit never stretched any further than rescuing a house, two cottages and Penruin, and many people thought me stark raving mad to attempt those.

At that time I was fascinated not only by the buildings but also by the whole business of selling them to the public. A simple enquiry at an estate agent's office was likely to be followed by half a day or more of being driven round the various possibilities in the agent's car. There were times when we felt that we had inspected every attic from Durham to Dorset and pushed our heads into every airing cupboard from Cornwall to Kent.

Agents tended to use much the same kind of phraseology when describing their wares whichever part of the country they operated in. It was interesting to see how they explained away the flowery eulogizing phrases in their descriptive leaflets when faced with a customer and the property at the same time. We became expert at translating the poetic descriptions into harsh reality and in understanding the precise meaning of every grunt and tut of probing surveyors. 'A much sought-after property' was likely to mean that it was so remote that it was very difficult to find. 'A unique residence' meant that one was not likely to have seen such a monstrosity before and, with a bit of luck, was unlikely to come across such a horror again. 'Easily maintained garden' meant that it was more or less non-existent and 'situated in a quiet backwater' meant that the place flooded every time it rained.

My publisher was also househunting at the same time and we would often swap stories of our adventures when we met. 'Why don't you do a humorous book on the subject?' he suggested, and I did. It was a small pocket-sized book called *A Place of Your Own* and was followed later by a larger volume called *This Desirable Plot – A Dreamhouse Hunter's Nightmare*. I have had a soft spot for house agents ever since – they bought those books in impressive numbers and many of them used drawings from them in their advertising matter for years afterwards. I saw two of them in an estate agent's window in Winchester only a few weeks ago.

Hampshire Cottages

We are, of course, all like drops of water in a vast surging river, or grains of sand on some ever-shifting beach, so that it is difficult to realize (particularly at the time) that we are unwittingly part of some great movement which as individuals we cannot control. It is difficult even now to appreciate that our house-hunting days were part of a great social and economic change which had started many years ago and was simply accelerated by the war. Villages everywhere had grown up over the centuries to house and serve the vast numbers of people who worked on the land. Their isolation, due to the difficulties of travel, had preserved a way of life which, although it was almost always hard, and usually uncomfortable, was nevertheless important to them and change was looked upon with suspicion and often with hostility. Although the industrial revolution had been responsible for a vast shift of population from the countryside to the industrial towns, the villages had still retained a good deal of their original purpose and had preserved insular attitudes which persisted until the invention of the internal combustion engine. The coming of the motor car brought an end to the isolation of the villages – even the more remote ones – and the tractors and other farm machines which quickly followed reduced the numbers of farm workers required on the land, so that many were forced to seek employment in the towns. The villages, which had been almost unchanged for hundreds of years, began to fall apart as self-contained units.

By the end of Hitler's war the rapid advance in new technology quickly put an end to the livelihood of most of the agricultural workers who still remained in the villages, hamlets and isolated cottages, and it became uneconomic to improve or even maintain many hundreds of rural properties. Large numbers were neglected and others were abandoned altogether and allowed to disintegrate. It was a chain reaction which ran through the greater part of our country areas. Not only the dwellings suffered; many local shops, smithies, schools and other establishments which served them became obsolete and were abandoned also. It was a sad state of affairs. The original purpose of our villages had almost gone and they were in mortal danger. The relatively small number of farm workers and country craftsmen who still lived there could rarely afford to repair and renovate their homes to the standard which the post-war generation had come to expect, even if they owned them, which they rarely did.

Inside every town dweller, however, is a countryman trying to get out and the partial vacuum which was created in the villages drew many of them inevitably back to where they felt (or imagined) their spiritual home to be. The money which they were able to earn in the towns enabled them to buy the empty and neglected country dwellings. The motor car which had started the dissolution enabled them to live in the country and continue to work in the towns. The pendulum was swinging back and the villages began to boom again, although not as the almost self-sufficient units they once were.

New problems inevitably arose, particularly where large numbers of cottages were used only as weekend retreats or holiday homes, so that the village became a neat, well-heeled ghost town for most of the week. It is not difficult to understand the resentment which often grew up in such communities against the 'townies' who were invading their domain. Young country people complained that when they married there were no homes left for them to buy or rent and that, in any case, the money offered by the newcomers for the poorest dwellings had forced prices up beyond their own limited range. It was a very real problem and, in many places, it still is.

On the credit side, however, most of those who bought rural property did so because they loved the country and were prepared to devote not only their money but their time and personal labour to the often daunting task of restoring and improving their new homes. In many places they brought fresh blood and a new vigour to the social activities of the communities. Paradoxically, they frequently became the most fiercely protective inhabitants of their villages and quickly formed powerful pressure groups to fight against destructive exploitation by outside interests.

The movement of population back to the countryside began gradually. As recently as fifteen to twenty years ago the rural areas were littered with damp, rotting and disintegrating buildings, but the movement back to the countryside has accelerated so much that it is difficult today to find buildings which have not already been taken in hand by someone.

Whatever social problems may have been created, the fact is that the villages, hamlets and cottages of Britain have never been in such good condition or so well maintained throughout their long history.

It seems to me that where social problems exist it would be wise for us to solve them as quickly as possible before the pendulum starts to swing back once more. Big movements of population are not, on the whole caused by greed or caprice on the part of individuals, but by changes in circumstance which we cannot easily control. If the worldwide problem of fuel shortage gets worse, which at the present time seems highly likely, then it may not be possible any longer for people to live more than a mile or two from their place of work. One cannot help but wonder what will happen then to the thousands of areas where virtually no work exists, either agricultural or industrial. I earnestly hope that the villages of Britain will not find themselves obsolete and deserted once more.

There is a great temptation to think of village life in the past in over-romanticized terms but it is a fatuous illusion to suppose that our forefathers lived in idyllic conditions of rural bliss. The contrary was the case. Before the eighteenth century, cottages of the kind we know today did not exist. The working population lived in huts and hovels and were little better off than beggars. Around the 1770s consciences were being stirred and voices raised in protest at their plight, but little was done about it.

Even then the rich were blinded by the picturesque quality which so many broken down hovels undoubtedly possess, particularly when set in sylvan surroundings. Efforts to design better dwellings were made by various architects from time to time but even they tended to be under the same romantic illusion and deliberately tried to ape the appearance of existing housing. So widespread was the cult of the picturesque that wealthy landowners frequently built cottages for their own use, although any resemblance to the real thing was purely superficial.

Methods of building and materials used naturally varied according to what was available locally so that some regions (the Cotswolds, for example, where good stone was cheap and plentiful) produced sounder structures than others. But as far as living conditions were concerned many cottages were little better than the original hovels. They remained, for the most part, cold, damp and insanitary, with floors of earth and walls built of mud and dung. So poor was the quality of the materials in many places that the entire structures collapsed into ruins in heavy rainstorms. Sanitation was almost non-existent.

A report produced about 1840 stated that the condition of rural dwellings was responsible for an alarmingly high death rate from fever. But the upper classes were still blinded by the cult of romanticism and mediaeval revivalism. Disease-ridden rural slums were accepted long after as natural and even desirable decorations of the countryside. Watercolour painting was very much in vogue as an accomplishment and landscapes tended to be considered incomplete without a thatched hovel as the focal point. As a landscape painter myself, I can understand how this came about and it is true, even today, that most people are attracted by such pictures. But it is inconceivable that it should have had any influence, however small, on attitudes to the conditions in which human beings were forced to live.

Other pressures, notably economic ones, had far more influence than the purely visual ones, however. At the beginning of the present century the majority of cottages had no drainage system whatsoever, so that refuse and slops were merely thrown out of doors. Earth closets often contaminated the soil, and water pumps and wells were frequently so badly sited that sewage leaked into them, causing sickness and death.

At a time when so many people are rightly alarmed at the crazy way we pollute and contaminate the earth in the name of progress, it is a little surprising to realize that a century ago there was hardly a river, brook or stream in the country which was not polluted by sewage of one kind or another. Frightening as our position is today, we may yet glean a little comfort from the fact that we are becoming aware of our problems and serious attempts are being made to resolve them before it is too late.

Whether we were aware of it or not, Rhona and I were a tiny part of this movement back to village life. We were in a better position than most others, in that we could live permanently in the country without the need to travel daily to the towns. As a large proportion of my work was concerned with country life in general it was possible to argue that it was the natural place for us to live. We were still invaders, however, in the sense that we were not directly contributing to local agriculture. Our own experience has been that the original natives of villages have been extremely friendly and hospitable, but when we first moved into the country we were aware that whatever one did with dwellings and their surrounding land was very much the concern of those neighbours, who regarded the village as their own.

The first village house we bought was extremely ugly. It had been for sale for three or four years without attracting a serious offer

Rose Cottage   60

either from the villagers or anyone else. When we first saw it we had been repelled by its mean appearance. It sat there on a hill looking like a rather small country workhouse; its gaunt facade had a brick porch of nightmare design and the window above was bricked up. We didn't bother to look any closer. We drove past it again more than a year later. The sun was shining. It was still for sale. The brick-work looked a warmer colour and I realized that if one ignored the porch and blind window and the tired-looking slate roof, the proportions were really rather good. When we walked up the hill we were struck by the beauty of the site. The old house overlooked the roofs of the village and gave a fine vista of the church spire among tall dark pines. Rooks circled above the treetop nests like pieces of burned paper swirling in the up-draught of a garden bonfire and there were long prospects of rolling green countryside between the trees. I took some snaps of the house with a small box camera and had a few extra prints made of each. It is quite possible to paint on photographs with opaque watercolour and it was a method I had found useful on previous occasions. When I painted out the porch and painted a new, wider structure in its place, put the blind window back in and tidied up the roof, the building was completely changed in appearance. It looked lower and wider and altogether more inviting.

We carried out these changes on the building itself after we bought it and added white shutters to the windows which helped the illusion of greater width. Even before any repair work was done to the main fabric or any modernization of the interior had taken place, we were approached by a number of people who asked whether we would be willing to sell it to them. Two of these applicants had looked over the house before and rejected it on the grounds of its dismal appearance.

It was, as I have said, a very different situation to the present day. Country property was not easy to sell. The villagers were well aware of the condition of buildings they had known all their lives and showed an understandable lack of interest in wanting to live in them.

There was a sloping orchard between the house and the lane, a kitchen garden behind it and a couple of acres of paddock to the north. There was also a pair of semi-detached cottages included in the package which, although they were occupied by three adults and two teenagers, were not in fit condition to house animals. They were very pretty, made of local brick and flint, and they added a great deal (far more than the house) to the picturesque quality of that part of the village. Yet the roof was entirely rotten and let water in like a sieve. The walls were damp and all woodwork was suffering from dry rot and woodworm. Sanitation was catered for by two tiny tumble-down earth closets outside. Both dwellings consisted of one room upstairs and one down connected by tiny, almost spiral staircases tucked tightly into the corners of the building, although the upper room of one cottage, occupied by a lady and her two teenage children (of different sexes), was divided by a studwork screen. Each had a small lean-to wooden shed with a tap, although only one had a sink. With electric light, these were the only signs of modern conveniences.

Although there was no question of us profiting in any way by owning these cottages, we were technically landlords and it caused us much worry and dismay. Both families had occupied the dwelling for many years and it was difficult to know how to act without seeming either to be interfering with their private lives or to be indifferent to their plight. I talked with several builders who refused flatly to have anything to do with work on the cottages. They were close to collapse, they said, and they were not prepared to risk life and limb by climbing on to the roof, much less by moving anything. I thought of making strong protests to the local authority and pointing out that the two families were in dire need of rehousing as an urgent priority. I did, in fact, do this after some hesitation and was relieved to find that the local authority agreed with me and said they were doing their best. I was, however, constantly worried that any great pressure on my part might be interpreted as an attempt to get the tenants out for my own convenience or profit. It was a situation which we had not desired nor would ever wish to find ourselves in again.

My peace of mind was not improved, either, by one of the

occupants, an inoffensive and friendly enough man with whom I often chatted in the evening over his garden gate. He never at any time made a comment about me buying the property but he would frequently nod towards another cottage on the other side of the lane which was in a similar state of dilapidation to his own. This heap of ruin and decay had also been bought by someone from outside the village, who eventually restored it to a delightful, sound and well-appointed home which was an asset rather than a liability to the whole community. 'That's the trouble, you see,' he would say. 'These people come along and buy up our homes and there's nothing left for the likes of us.' There was no rancour in the man, however, and although I knew he was obliquely referring to me as well as to a number of other newcomers, it was still possible to get round the subject with a smile and a nod and we always remained on the best of terms.

We were seriously worried, however, about his wife who was in bad health. We could not bear to think of the conditions in which she lived, and yet we were unable to do anything about them. At that time we were renewing the roof of our own house and modernizing the antiquated facilities within. There was, in consequence, a yard full of building materials – bricks, slates, tiles and many household objects such as pipes, taps, a bath, two deep white ceramic sinks, lavatory basins, etc., which, if old-fashioned, were nonetheless in excellent condition. They lay near to the end of my neighbour's garden not more than fifty paces at most from his cottage door. Unlike his wife, he seemed in excellent health and was only in his middle years.

'Why don't you take one of these sinks?' I said to him one day. 'There are plenty of bricks, too, which you are welcome to and the builders mix new cement almost every day. If you did it one Saturday morning you could build two brick plinths and have a sink in place for your wife before midday. All the fittings are there to carry the water away through the wall.' He looked mildly shocked. 'You can take any materials you wish, including ready mixed cement and mortar,' I continued. 'It won't cost you anything and if you give me a shout I'll give you a hand to carry the things.'

He shuffled his feet a bit and said, 'We've only got a bucket under the tap, you know. What can you do when you've only got a bucket under the tap?'

'Put a sink under it,' I said.

He kicked idly at a section of ivy-covered flint walling which divided his garden from mine. 'A chap died jumping off that wall some years ago,' he said, and the subject of the sink was never mentioned again. His shiftlessness rather angered me at first, but I knew the appalling conditions in which he and his wife had lived for many years and came to wonder whether if I had lived in such circumstances I might not also have been reduced to total apathy.

No, the cottage homes of England were never an earthly paradise.

To our great relief, and I'm sure to theirs, both families were rehoused eventually and the local authority issued a demolition order on the cottages. I did not understand why this was done so quickly after they became vacant, until a number of persons from outside the village called at the house and pleaded with us to let them occupy the premises temporarily. It was obviously out of the question to allow such a hovel to be lived in again and the demolition order put a quick end to argument.

All the same it seemed a pity to sweep the cottages away without thought. Unfit for human habitation they certainly were, yet they had great charm and looked so right where they stood. They belonged to their surroundings just as Penruin did, so I asked for a year's stay of execution in order to think about them and it was granted. Rhona and I worked almost every evening during that year making plans and drawings of what might possibly be done to avoid demolition. It needed no professional eye to see that the only part which could possibly be saved was the outer walls. The cottages were also too small to be of much use as convenient dwellings and would have to be considerably enlarged. The difficulty lay in how to do that without losing their character. It was not such an easy matter for I had seen a number of attempts to enlarge old properties by sticking new pieces on and the result was almost always a disaster. One such example resembled a railway accident. It looked as if a modern diesel locomotive had crashed into the side of an old steam engine. Some other answer had to be found.

I was anxious to carry out any new work in exactly the same style and with the same materials. The existing building was of flint with a general framework of soft red brick and both of these items were readily available locally – but there was a snag. Obviously all new work would have to conform to modern standards which, among other details, included cavity walls. The trouble was that I could not find a builder anywhere who had ever built cavity walls of flint. Most of them said it was out of the question; not possible. Some clearly thought I was some kind of looney. Luckily I met a builder who took an entirely different view. He had never heard of it being done before, he said, but was willing to have a go if I was. I certainly was so he had a go and it was entirely successful. The interior layer of the walling was of course built in the accepted modern manner and the outer skin was built of flints which were laid with mortar inside wooden shuttering. Wire wall-ties were inserted in the usual manner. Provided that no more than a maximum of two feet depth of flints was laid at a time and the shuttering was left in place for a day or two, before being raised to take the next section, the work was quite straightforward. I do not recollect that we met any real difficulties at all.

When the wooden support was moved upwards it left a strip of wall which looked very messy because the mortar had spread over most of the flint facing. The mortar had, however, reached a 'green' stage by then which meant that, although it was firm and strong, it had not become really hard and it was possible to cut, carve or scrape it not only with ease but also with great pleasure. I could hardly wait to finish my own work and get outside to work on the latest exposed section of wall. I can recommend cutting green mortar off a flint wall as one of the most absorbing and relaxing occupations of all time. Rhona and the children tried it, too, and from then on there was keen competition to be first at the next section of exposed wall. The best tool for doing the job is a six-inch nail grasped firmly in the hand with the head used as the cutting blade. Not only is the mortar easy to carve at this stage but as each flint emerges it becomes an individual work of art. No two are quite the same in shape or colour but as the work proceeds they blend together to produce the most beautiful texture. It is one of the few occupations in life where one cannot possibly lose, for the disappointment of finding that there are no more flints to attend to is offset by the thrill of seeing a completed wall which is a work of art and a joy forever. Tom Sawyer's friends took no more delight in whitewashing his aunt's wooden fence than we did in working on those walls and we didn't have to bribe the builders to let us do it.

Our daughter, Penny, had collected one or two stones from each place she had been to since infancy as souvenirs and she kept them in her bedroom, exhibited like a collection of fine jewels. The lure of the walls, however, was too much for her and one by one she produced her treasures to be incorporated in the pattern. When the job was done she was able to point out each of her own stones and recount its history – which she frequently did. It was a heartwarming example of a little girl giving up her own treasures for the delight of others – until the day we were leaving and she asked for her stones back. We dried her tears and explained that however loud she screamed the stones could not be recovered, but she still had a go at those she could reach.

During the building of the walls one of the workmen accidentally dropped a large flint from the scaffolding on to the stockpile below and it split cleanly into two halves as if it had been cut with a knife. In the very centre was a perfectly spherical cavity about three quarters of an inch across (presumably a million-year-old bubble). At no point was it nearer than three inches to the outer surface of the flint and when I examined it, in spite of the impact it had suffered, there were a few small pieces of moss and a spider inside the hollow. They were dark brown (almost black), dry as dust and light as gossamer but the forms were unmistakable.

The finished design of the cottage was pleasantly irregular in shape. Roofing it was as intriguing an adventure as solving the problem of the walls. Although the original dwellings had been roofed in grey slate it was the only feature that did not conform to the local tradition. Most cottages which were not thatched were roofed with warm red tiles, hand made and pleasantly textured.

Don Chambers came to our aid here, for at that time much country and village property was being demolished and tens of thousands of these ancient and beautiful tiles were being thrown from the roofs to explode into powder on the debris below. As an architect, Don knew where such demolitions were taking place and arranged for me to obtain twenty-two thousand of them which we stacked in the garden. It seemed an awful lot but when work on the roofs were completed there were no more than two or three thousand tiles left over. I preserved them carefully, however, and have put the rest of them to good use since then. They were made in 1788. I found one on which this date had been cut on the wet clay. The names of two men (presumably the tile makers) were also on the same tile. On another one was a simple sum which may well have been an addition of the wages list for the week. They were venerable tiles, there is no doubt, but the spider must have been snug inside his stone bubble for aeons when James Brown and William Fance signed their handiwork, and the Bastille was still unstormed.

There is no doubt that that cottage was the most complete and satisfying job I have ever done on a building, for it was within our own land and we were able to take time. We had few of the difficulties and frustrations which we encountered later at Penruin. It was the first place where I was able to make a water garden of any size which, in addition to being a great visual asset, was invaluable in that it collected most of the water from the saturated slope of the hillside and channelled it away past the cottage into the roadside ditch.

Our children spent most of their childhood there in the house and later in the cottage and, like us, they remember the place with great affection. A number of our friends were puzzled (some still are) by why we were content to do so much work on various places, live there for a time and then move on, for the property boom did not get under way until after we had left Penruin. The fact is that profit in a monetary sense had nothing to do with it. We simply liked taking over a building which had been rejected by others and trying to bring out its real potential. It seemed to us that any money we could save was better converted into something we could see and enjoy rather than into figures in a little green book. It is not possible to do anything without taking some risks but although there was little or no profit in it, if we took our own labour into account, we were fairly confident that we could recover our outlay if the need arose.

We did lose a little when we left Penruin, for General de Gaulle had cornered all the gold or lead or something at the time and there was some sort of financial crisis. But overall we broke about even and in the process we amassed vast profits in enjoyment. There is enormous satisfaction in making something beautiful or restoring something which was once so, particularly when it is likely to give pleasure for another hundred years and be useful into the bargain.

Circumstances over which we had no control made it impossible for us to live permanently at Penruin or even to remain there as long as we would have needed to complete the work we started, but we have never regretted our involvement with the place for one single moment.

When we first saw it it was a beautiful ruin. When we left it it was still as picturesque but was a ruin no longer. We did not restore it as fully as we would have wished but we stopped the rot in more ways than one and set it on its feet again as a most attractive house.

Penruin will no doubt continue to change in various ways and, hopefully, it may become even more attractive than ever before, but to me it will always remain as it was that April morning when the wild daffodils were blowing by the orchard spring, when a kingfisher perched upon a spray of hawthorn and a caddis fly trundled his house across a smooth white pebble.

It seems no longer than a few fleeting moments to me since I left the mill for the last time; quiet, beautiful and obsolete, it stood in that far away wooded valley, and yet the world has already turned about since then to face the direction from whence it came. I saw a scientist last night on television, explaining how the world must seek new answers to the problem of survival when the fossil fuels have gone forever.

He was demonstrating a strangely familiar kind of wheel which, he said, could be used to harness the power of water.